**Books should be returned or renewed by the
last date stamped above**

Awarded for excellence
to Arts & Libraries

Kent
County
Council

ISBN 0–9544519–0–2

First published 2003
Reprinted 2004
Copyright © Ray Lambert, 2003, 2004

Published by: RAYL, 13 Weedswood Road, Chatham, Kent ME5 0QR

Contents

Prologue   1

Chapter 1   3

Chapter 2   12

Chapter 3   24

Chapter 4   36

Chapter 5   45

Chapter 6   54

Chapter 7   64

Chapter 8   75

Chapter 9   85

Chapter 10   95

Chapter 11   100

Chapter 12   108

Chapter 13   118

Chapter 14   128

Chapter 15   138

PROLOGUE

As you will gather from the following pages, I was a 'Ganges Inmate' for the year that straddled the winter of 1953, or to be more precise: May 1953 to June 1954.

It was hell. I don't say that for dramatic effect, it really was hell. Or, in the interests of accuracy, as near as I could imagine hell to be.

Nothing was ever right; whatever one did, someone would be on hand to shout at you for getting it wrong. I can only speak with authority about the year that I endured but I can see no reason why any other year should have been much different.

They took young boys straight from home and then inflicted every kind of hardship, humiliation and mental anguish they could think of upon them. Something they had perfected over the years since the place had first opened. Indeed even before that. Their basic 'craft' was practiced on the old HMS Ganges, before she transferred her name and her 'cargo' to the Shotley Peninsula in 1905.

Boys applied to join the Navy but there was never any mention of the hardships they would endure on their way to becoming sailors. Those perpetually smiling recruiters could fill a boys head with all kinds of good feelings, but why was it they never mentioned Ganges—and why was it they were continually smiling?

It was one elaborate con trick really. Young boys were obliged to sign on the dotted line long before they ever set eyes on the place. Then they were packed off to Shotley.

By the time it dawned on them what they had done, it was too late. All they were left with was the vision of twelve long years stretching out ahead of them and in more immediate terms, the twelve long months of sheer purgatory stretching out ahead of them at Ganges.

There were good times; I've been told there were good times. My personal recollections of good times are not enough to cover the fingers of one hand. There were good times; there must have been. I must have missed them.

I am a storyteller. What I have attempted to do is tell a story. The story of my time at HMS Ganges.

My story does not dwell on the good times, because there wasn't that many. My story does not dwell upon the hardships, although they were real enough.

I have tried to catalogue the events that happened to me, or around me, during my time at Shotley. Bad times; good times; sad times and the occasional

1

happy times are all there.

Some of the stories have been embellished with a bit of writers licence but the events depicted are true. The names of the characters have been changed to protect the guilty.

Chief Bumble, PO Jury, Humph the boxer, Puck, Jasper, Dereham, Leeward, Raines, Southern, Lowley, Daisy and others are all real people sheltering under a *nom de plume*. The central character shouldn't be difficult to figure out. I recall them all with nostalgia.

I freely admit that this book is a personal indulgence, as I would expect most books are. However, I hope I have been objective enough to make my story interesting for all tastes.

May it give as much pleasure in the reading as it did in the writing.

Chapter 1

'Fall in three deep,' yelled someone.

Young Raymond, a fresh faced, ginger-haired, fifteen year old from the Norfolk villages was in his element. He knew exactly what that meant, having spent some time attached to the Army Cadets back home. The Army said three ranks actually, but the message was loud and clear and he was eager to impress.

He and a crowd of young lads all of a similar age had just spilled out of the train at Ipswich station, on their first step toward a career with the Royal Navy.

If someone at that moment had asked him what he was doing there, he would have been hard pressed to come up with a satisfactory answer. In fact, although he hadn't realised it himself at this stage, he didn't know what he was doing there.

His introduction to the Senior Service had been simple enough. Sitting at home one day he had been idly thumbing through an old magazine wondering what to do when he left school in a few months time, when a Royal Navy advertisement caught his eye. It showed a couple of blokes in tropical whites in a motorboat, alongside the gangway of an aircraft carrier. It was an idyllic scene and just the thing to catch a young mans attention.

JUST SEND THE COUPON FOR A FREE BOOK, screamed the words underneath the picture and that was all the encouragement required to produce scissors and start a whole chain of events into action. With the free book came an innocent looking form with an invitation to '.... fill in a few particulars about yourself.'

This in turn led to an invitation to go to the Norwich Recruiting Office for an informal chat and from there it was an easy step to '.... just try the test.... to see how you get on.'

Despite young Raymond's bashful protests about not being very good at sums, the ever smiling recruiter was soon patting him on the back and assuring him with well worn phrases like: 'You're too modest son .... you've done very well .... just the sort of chap the Navy needs.'

That recruiter had used the same routine many times before, but those words were like music to young Raymond's ears. People in authority and complete strangers to boot had actually treated him like a man, with kindness and respect. That, plus 'doing so well' on the test had done miracles for his ego and a very proud young man swaggered from the Recruiting Office on that February afternoon and almost floated to the station where he could hardly wait to catch the train home to tell his parents how clever the man said he was.

Soon after, a letter arrived offering a free trip to London to undergo a full serviceman's medical and, without a thought for the consequences, was eagerly snapped up. He had only been to London once before and that was on a day trip to the zoo with his school, but this time it was different, now he was a man and he was going on his own. Anyway his father, always the eternal pessimist, had said over and over again that he would never pass the strict medical examination, which made him even more determined to prove that he could.

'Come on Ginger, look sharp.'

Those words snapped him out of his thoughts and back to reality.

'Well come on then. Pick up your case and get moving.'

Slightly embarrassed at having been caught napping, he quickly picked up his suitcase and joined the line of boys who were moving slowly toward the door of a coach the Navy had sent to meet them off the train.

That was the first time he had ever been addressed as Ginger. His mother had always insisted that he was called Raymond. She wouldn't tolerate anything else. Anyone who deviated was firmly put in their place. Even Ray was not good enough.

'His name is Raymond,' she would snap without the least deference to status or politeness.

But Ginger, yes he liked Ginger; it was new and, he felt, it suited him. His mother certainly would not have approved but she wasn't there. He was a man now, a man making his own decisions. From now on his name would be Ginger; it had a man-of-the-world ring to it.

Once seated on the coach and they headed out of town toward Shotley, which was to be their home for the next twelve months, his mind drifted back once more to the events that led him here and how happy he had been when he proved his father wrong by passing the service medical in London, with flying colours.

The medical was never a problem in any case; it was just an incidental on a day trip to London. Apart from his mother insisting upon him wearing clean underwear, the question of the medical examination never entered his head. No, the worry if indeed worry came into it at all, was how to find his way around London on his own, bearing in mind this would be his first solo trip.

However, fate took a hand at this stage and dealt him an incredible bit of good fortune.

An old school mate, 'Blondie' Biscuit, who was slightly older and had already joined the army, was home on leave and was due to go back to his barracks on the same day as Raymond's London trip. Blondie, now being a man of the world and an accomplished London traveller, agreed to show him the way to the appointed place in Whitehall, so the problem of getting lost never actually materialised. The thought suddenly struck him: throughout their school years, his mother had never voiced an opinion about the Biscuit family calling their son Blondie. That appeared to be all right for them but no such thing for her son would be allowed.

Medical passed and London negotiated all in the same day was quite a feather in his cap and something to boast to his pals about. Whether they were impressed or not was hard to tell, but who cared anyway. Somehow he felt different; he felt he had grown up overnight. Now he was a man and soon he would be travelling the world just like those blokes in that Navy advertisement.

There was not much left to do but wait for the postman to bring an envelope marked OHMS, which, hopefully, would bring details of his joining up date. The waiting seemed to go on forever, but still without a thought for what he was letting himself in for, Raymond's eagerness grew stronger as the days passed and the advice of his pals 'not to go' just served to make him that much more determined.

The anticipated notification duly arrived and, on the appointed day, he took the local train to Norwich where he met up with several others of the same age, then en-bloc they boarded the train for Ipswich.

His mind drifted back just in time for him to see the gates of the Annexe loom up as the coach turned right, off the main road, then right again as it trundled through to the small induction centre parade ground. He didn't know what 'The Annexe' was; in fact at that moment he had no idea what anything was. It was early days yet but, as they alighted from the coach and got their first sight of the place, one thing was certain—like it or not, he had arrived.

The coach had come to a halt outside the New Entries Divisional Office and straight away the passengers began filing out of the door and congregating on the parade ground. Some of them, former sea cadets probably, he thought, immediately assumed the air of old hands; a few others looked close to tears.

'Fall in three deep', a disembodied voice bellowed and straightaway they began shuffling about into some semblance of three ranks, a routine that was already becoming familiar to them. Having sorted themselves out into three straight lines, Raymond—or Ginger, as he now intended to be known—began to take in his surroundings.

They were standing outside the Divisional Office, a small, single story building with a flagpole in front. Adjoining the office and to the left, was the sick bay. These buildings were on one end of the rectangular parade ground and directly opposite, at the far end, was the dining hall. The two long sides of the rectangle were taken up by a continuous single story covered walkway, about ten feet wide, open fronted apart from wooden struts set at intervals, which were supporting the corrugated tin roof. Although he didn't realise it at the time, behind that walkway were the barrack rooms that they would inhabit for the next six weeks.

By now the place seemed full of people in uniform strutting about very impressively. They all appeared to be talking at once and, as far as he could make out, to no-one in particular.

They certainly didn't appear to be achieving anything, although someone must have known what was happening, he reasoned. Then suddenly one of the gaggle of officials addressed them.

'Right then, answer your names when they're called.'

Now they were under way. The first batch of names were called and soon after that crowd of boys were moved away. Then came the second lot and the new Ginger's was the fourth name called. Soon that second batch was complete and they were moved away to their new home—Jellico Two mess. Jellico Two was the second hut along under the right hand walkway and was under the control of chief Bumble, a thin, dapper man who looked like and walked like a little bantam cock. Once inside the hut Bumble started fussing about allocating numbers and assigning beds according to those numbers. As Ginger was number four, he had the fourth bed on the left inside the door.

He was one of the first to be allocated which gave him plenty of time to look around, collect his thoughts and take stock of the place while the remainder of his new messmates was being shown to their beds and lockers.

The room, or mess, as it had to be called—'You're in the Navy now lad. Learn to use naval terms'—was a long dormitory type place with beds along each side at right angles to the walls and a couple of long wooden tables up the centre.

By now Bumble had finished matching people to beds and a motley crew of assorted lads in all modes of dress, ranging from someone in a woollie jumper and plimsoles to someone in what looked like a brand new suit and all variations in between, were standing at the foot of their respective beds and, for the first time since they got off the train at Ipswich station, there was complete silence.

Looking at the line of faces opposite young Ginger could see that homesickness had already taken over in several cases and there was little doubt that if someone had offered a ride back to the station at that moment,

6

there would have been sighs of relief all around and a mass exodus from Jellico Two mess—and quite possibly every other mess in the place.

There were still no thoughts of the future for him though. All he had on his mind was what was happening right now. It had all been a great adventure for the young country boy; a bit like a day out with the army cadets that he had enjoyed not so very long ago.

Chief Bumble had the business of new intakes off to a fine art. Without realising it, the new boys had negotiated their first day in the Navy. There had been something to do at all times, although very little, if anything at all, had actually been done.

He had kept Jellico Two mess occupants entertained somehow since their arrival on that coach. There had been a little talk about naval traditions and why some things were done in a particular manner instead of the obvious easy way.

'That's the Navy way and the quicker you get that into your heads, the easier things will be for you.'

If there was two ways to do anything, even the most mundane everyday thing, then there seemed to be an obsession to use the most back to front, cack-handed way rather than just go to it, straight forward.

They were soon to learn.

Another little pearl of wisdom that was to help them enormously throughout those early days was imparted by Bumble, that first afternoon.

'I am a chief petty officer telegraphist, but you will not call me chief. You will address me as 'sir' at all times. Is that perfectly clear?'

'In fact, while I'm at it, you will address all instructors and staff as sir and then we shall get along famously.'

This was probably a line he used with all new recruits as they came under his charge. He seemed to know exactly what he was saying and he left the new boys in no doubt as to what he meant.

Quite possibly this was never intended as a friendly word to the wise, but more likely was just a personal ego trip. Either way those that remembered were grateful because it saved them the public humiliation of being screamed at in front of all and sundry, for addressing an instructor as 'mister' or worse still as 'oy'.

Chief Bumble wasn't too bad really, as instructors went. The new recruits didn't know that of course; they had nothing to judge him by; they had never come across a situation like this before. Everything and everybody seemed incredibly bad and the whole place was run very strictly, just like they imagined the inside of the tougher kind of prison to be.

Bumble had managed to keep them occupied through those first few hours together in their new home and now it was supper time and time to have their first meal together.

'Right then lads. Fall in outside ready to march over to the dining hall.'

The boys obediently filed out onto the parade ground and formed themselves into three ranks facing Jellico Two mess, just as if it was the most natural thing in the world although, for the majority of them, this was only the third time they had been called upon to perform such an operation. Already their young minds were adapting to their new environment and such manoeuvres were becoming a matter-of-fact everyday routine that they did with very little thought; service routine was already becoming part of everyday life.

By this time the remainder of the new intake was all doing likewise until everyone was on the parade ground, in three ranks facing their respective messes. Then they were marched off to the dining hall where each mess had their own allocated tables. Chief Bumble guided his charges to their correct tables and all other instructors were doing the same with their flocks.

It was very early days and the boys had not learned that the Navy likes everything done in complete silence, so their first entrance was a complete shambles, in naval terms, as the boys chatted away with each other probably subconsciously glad that the pressure was off for a while and they were back to something like a familiar routine, one that most of them was performing every day not so long ago, back at school.

'You're duty cook lad,' Bumble shouted above the din.

Those few words were like a smack in the face for Ginger. The smile dropped from his face; all thoughts from the immediate past drained from his mind. He felt quite ill. His legs trembled and the blood roared in his ears. Cook. He didn't want to be a cook. He knew nothing about cooking. This was a bit sudden; he grabbed the edge of the table for support. Nobody had mentioned anything about cooking before.

'But sir, I can't cook,' he mumbled, almost in tears. He wanted to say more but was not sure that he could control himself. He wanted to be a sailor not a cook, but crying like a baby, a situation he felt very near to, wouldn't help anything. Anyway how would it look, bursting into tears in front of all this lot.

He had come there to be a man and he had to try to act like one. He gulped hard and tried to compose himself as his reeling senses slowed down. He gulped again and pretended to cough to give himself a bit more time.

'But sir,' he began again. He felt hot and his eyes were full of tears, 'I, I, I, er, this cooking,' he was gulping like mad and looked round self consciously to see who was watching him squirm. But everything was going on just as before, no-one was looking at him. Apparently nobody had noticed his near collapse and this brought some of his confidence back. Coughing again to disguise the fact he was brushing a tear from the end of his nose, he now felt confident enough to face Bumble and try to persuade him to pick someone else.

'Sir, I'm afraid I ....'

Bumble wasn't listening; he hadn't heard a word that Ginger had said. He wasn't even looking at him.

'Come on then lad, you ready?' he said, turning abruptly and walking away.

Ginger's first thoughts were to pretend he didn't know Bumble was addressing him. But no, that was too easy. The other boys were beginning to sort themselves out and sit down so he would certainly be singled out again and this time other people would be listening.

'Sir, sir, but sir ....' he caught up with Bumble at the serving hatch at the bottom end of the dining hall. 'I don't know anything about having to be a cook.' His composure had returned now although he still had that sickening feeling.

'Of course not lad, that's what I'm here for, to show you what to do. Just wait here in line until it's your turn at the counter.'

Well at least that's a relief. Bumble was going to stay with him. He would be able to do the talking; they would listen to him. Bumble would explain that this new lad wasn't a cook. The panic had all left young Ginger now and he felt brave enough to try on a mild argument, in the hope of supplying Bumble with some ammunition to use in his defence.

'This cooking business sir: I don't know much about cooking. I didn't know I would have to do the cooking.'

'Cooking lad? You haven't got to do any cooking. We have qualified chefs to do all that. All you have to do is pick up the meals and serve your table, then when the meal is over you pick up the empty plates and take them back to where you collected them. After that you just wipe off your table, that's all. That's not too difficult is it?'

What a relief. Ginger could have danced for joy; so he wasn't to be a cook after all. Duty cook was another of those stupid naval terms that had nothing to do with cooking.

Bumble was like a guardian angel. He hadn't noticed Ginger's agitated state, apparently. They just stood side by side in silence until it was their turn at the serving hatch, then Bumble broke the silence between them.

'OK lad pick up a basket.'

The basket was a wire framework contraption designed to hold eight plates, four either side of the carrying handle. Into this Ginger slipped eight plates of food and carried them back to the head of his table, where they were passed along to hungry boys and annihilated in seconds. The wrench of leaving home for the first time hadn't affected their appetites.

Being the last one to sit down to eat, after having passed the other seven plates along the table, he was a bit behind the others and by the time he had polished off his fish and chips, which were cold anyway, they had gone leaving him to pick up the empty plates and wipe off the table top.

The task of serving meals and cleaning up after was almost a pleasure compared to what he thought he had to do and Ginger went to it, if not exactly with enjoyment then certainly happy in the knowledge that his term as 'duty cook' would soon be over. It was just a pity that he was singled on the first day, on his very first meal. However, the shock had passed now and after finishing off his chores he made his way back to Jellico Two mess a lot happier than he had been twenty minutes earlier.

As he entered the mess Bumble was there and still waffling on like he had been all afternoon. Although he could be a bit snappy, he wasn't too bad really.

He had kept them occupied throughout their first few hours together and then he had guided them through their first meal together and now, as Ginger came in, he was insisting that everyone write a letter home.

'Now I know a lot of you are feeling homesick,' he was saying as Ginger approached. 'After all that is only natural, but don't tell your mum that because by the time she gets your letter you will have settled in and then your letter will sound very childish.'

Bumble had a heart; he probably had a mother. For an instructor he had a deep understanding of compassion. Ginger conceded that Bumble was quite probably right and he knew perfectly well that his father would just love him to say that he'd made a mistake. But despite Bumbles advice, he still told his mum he was beginning to regret his decision to join up.

The Navy wasn't all it was cracked up to be. I bet those blokes in their tropical whites in that advertisement didn't have all this hassle on their first day, he thought to himself.

By the time the letters were written it was time for bed. It was only about nine o'clock and they were men now. It was May and it was still light outside. The boys back home would still be out on the sports field or riding their bikes about, but Bumble was treating them like children. Perhaps in the bustle of the first day he had overlooked the fact that they had all left school and had come there of their own free will to be sailors. They were men now.

Perhaps it was another of those Navy ways. After all it was their first day.

Perhaps the Navy thought they would be tired after their journey. Yes, that must be it.

Things would settle down later into a proper serviceman's routine. Tomorrow probably. When they got kitted out with their new uniforms, then things would be different. They wouldn't stand out so much and look so new when they got their uniforms. In the evenings they would go to the canteen for a game of darts or maybe some of them would go into town, to the pictures or something. Maybe they would impress the local girls in their new blue suits. Yes, he was looking forward to going to town in his new uniform.

Whatever they did they certainly wouldn't be in bed by nine o'clock, that's for sure. Whatever would the boys back home think of it. In bed by nine o'clock indeed. He resolved to look into it in the morning, just to put these Navy people right and establish just what the procedure was.

Was he in for a shock—if only he could have known.

'Towel over your arm, soap and flannel, down to the wash room for a wash and then back here as quickly as you can. Right, away you go then.'

Although things were not going quite as Ginger had anticipated, he was still eager to impress Bumble. He was the first back from the washroom and quickly hanging his towel over the foot of his bed, he stood proudly 'at ease' alongside it, just like the army cadets had taught him.

'You're back quick lad, have you cleaned your teeth?'

'Er .... no sir,' suddenly he wasn't quite so proud.

'Well get 'an do it then, 'stead of standing there grinning like a bloody Cheshire Cat.'

Bumbles compassion from the dining hall had apparently deserted him.

When everyone was back from having a wash and all towels were hanging neatly over the foot of respective beds, to Bumbles satisfaction, He went to turn out the lights.

'Well goodnight lads, time to get some sleep. I know a lot of you are feeling a bit homesick, don't be afraid of shedding a few tears into your pillow, it's nothing to be ashamed of. I admit I did it on my first night.'

Ginger had had enough. The events of the day were catching up with him. What with his near heart attack in the dining hall and then being called 'a bloody Cheshire Cat' when all he was trying to do was impress and now being put to bed at nine o'clock like children, was all to much. He'd really had enough for one day.

From the comparative safety of under his blankets he mumbled:

'Aw, get stuffed Bumble. I've gone right off you ....'

Chapter 2

If there was one thing the Navy would not tolerate—above the scores of things the Navy would not tolerate—was people improperly dressed. Or to put it into the newly acquired service jargon, 'out of the rig of the day.' So 'nozzers', as all new entry boys were called, walking about in all manner of slovenliness, just as they had arrived from home, was certainly not to be tolerated.

Therefore the immediate priority was to get the latest intake over to the clothing store and get them kitted out with a uniform.

The clothing store was on the opposite side of the parade ground from Jellico Two and tacked onto the right hand end of the Divisional Office block.

So, straight after breakfast the following morning, the start of their first full day in the place, they were marched over, to wait outside the clothing store door. When the door was opened it exposed a long counter to their left that stretched away into the distance, the full length of the building and ended up at the far end next to another door. Behind the counter were several 'Jack Dusties' who's job it was to issue the kit—and, of course, the chief in charge.

'Right then, single file. In this door and out the other with a full kit. Look lively then.'

Easier said than done. The first stop inside the door was a kitbag. So far so good. Bang went the folded kitbag on the counter.

'Come on then, move along. Next.'

Of course, at this stage the obvious thing to do would be to open the kitbag and put the remainder of the kit inside, as it was supplied along the counter, on the way to the door at the other end.

But oh no, that was not the Navy way. The kitbag would remain folded and used like a tray, with everything else piled up on top. When you reached the far end of the line loaded up so high that you couldn't see over the top—then you could stow everything inside.

Yes, easier said than done.

As the end of the line was reached so the counter stopped. How does one take an enormous pile of kit and put it inside the kitbag, when there is nowhere to put it down and the kitbag is serving as a tray holding the remainder of the stuff that has to go inside it anyway? But that was yet to come. First they must run the gauntlet of Jack Dusties.

'What's yer shoe size?'

'I .... er ....'

Bang, bang. Too late. Two pairs of boots. 'Move along.'

'Inside leg?'

'I .... er ....'

Bang, bang, bang. Too late. Three suits. 'Move along.'

Socks, stockings, lanyards, handkerchiefs, mug, gloves, brushes shoe, brushes clothes, brushes hair, brushes tooth. Well at least that was straight forward.

'Collar size?'

'Well I'm afraid I don't .... '

Bang, bang. Too late. Two shirts No.8. 'Move along.'

I'm getting the hang of this now.

'Hat size?'

Oh sod it. I wasn't ready for that one. I'd never had a hat so I don't know.

'I don't know. Could I try on .... '

Bang, too late. Tin hat box and three hats, two black and one white.

'Move along. Next.'

Funnily enough most of the stuff they issued seemed to fit. They were either psychic, downright lucky or good at their job. Ginger grudgingly conceded that the kit issue had gone pretty well considering and back in Jellico Two again, when they had to try on all their new clothes, they at least took on the appearance of sailors and some of them actually began to feel that they belonged.

Now that everyone had been issued with a full kit everything, but everything, had to be clearly marked with the owners name and to this end each boy was supplied with a type.

A type was made of small blocks of wood, about three quarters of an inch square and about three inches long. On the end of each block was carved a letter; these blocks were fixed together to spell each individuals name. Every boy was issued a type as part of his kit.

Quite why it was called a type was anyone's guess. It was probably just another of those obscure Navy ways. It bore no resemblance to a typewriter although to some degree it did resemble the individual type used by newspapers.

Anyway, whatever the reasons, a 'type' it was and like the rest of the newly issued kit, it became each boys personal property to be accounted for at all times.

The next step then was to get the kit marked with the owner's name. This proved to be no easy task. Like everything else undertaken it was turned into a major evolution.

Every single item of kit had to be stamped; the dark colours with white and the lighter shades and the whites done in black.

To this end chief Bumble had two trays on the table in front of him. Each tray had an old piece of serge folded in it, one with white paint tipped over it, the other with black. The serge folded in the paint made a kind of pad similar to a rubber stamp pad and this was how they marked their kit, by dipping the type into the pad.

Every single item of kit had to be marked and what could not be done with paint—like boots and brushes—were stamped with metal letter punches. The only exception was the enamel mug, this escaped the ritual by having a stamped disc attached to the handle.

The thought crossed Ginger's mind that they seemed to be going well over the top with this marking business. Everything had to be marked in a certain sequence and in a certain place on each particular article and in the colour prescribed. Nothing was left out. Socks, gloves and even handkerchiefs had to have the treatment. It's a wonder they don't expect us to mark our name on the type as well, he reflected gloomily.

But that was not the end of the saga. All the marking had to be done, under Bumbles supervision, in a room next to the clothing store and then the kit had to be transported back to Jellico Two without smudging the newly marked name or getting paint on anything other than where it should be.

Then, the following day, as soon as the paint was dry, all names had to be embroidered over in chain stitch using red silk.

This operation took up all their time and seemed to go on forever, particularly as the vast majority of them had never done any kind of needlework before. Then there was the ever present additional hazard of knowing that anything not done up to standard was ordered to be picked out and redone more neatly. Ginger was envious of Sim and Lee who got away lightly with the sewing but he was glad his name wasn't MacSweeney or Arrowsmith, those two had almost twice as much to do as most of them.

But their eagerness to get the nozzers into uniform at the earliest possible moment, left a serious flaw in the Navy's carefully laid plans.

Because, somewhere back in the good old days, the powers that be, in their wisdom and for reasons known only to themselves, had decreed that all recruits should conform to a basic standard of appearance and dress and this over the years had become yet another of those obscure naval traditions that everyone kept trotting out all the time, but no-one really knew why.

Therefore—according to tradition—the next step to becoming a sailor was a visit to the pussers barber. Pussers being a term used in the Navy to describe anything to do with, or belonging to, the Navy. Again, like everything else in the boys early days, this was conducted like a major evolution. Nothing was left to chance. The entire inhabitants of Jellico Two mess were marched round to the barbers shop, so there was no way of avoiding the dreaded haircut.

The barbers shop was in a makeshift space next to the dining hall and although it was a bit primitive, it looked just like any other barbers shop that Ginger had ever seen except he thought there appeared to be far more hair laying about on the floor than where he had previously had his hair cut. The boys were ushered in three at a time, to take their place on one of the three vacant chairs—then it was that any resemblance to a civilised haircut vanished. He had taken a great deal of care with his hair. He had allowed it to grow quite long, into one of the modern styles that were just becoming fashionable. Naturally he expected to have it trimmed up a bit and although he wasn't too happy at the prospect, he conceded that servicemen's hair was fairly short. But he didn't expect the kind of treatment he received when it was his turn in the chair.

Having what was considered extraordinary long hair, particularly by Navy standards, he was immediately centre of attention as his barber did his best to ridicule him with loud sarcastic remarks to his colleagues, who were enjoying the impromptu entertainment.

'We don't get many ladies in here, do we boys .... didn't think pigtails were still legal in the Navy .... would you like a perm madam' Ginger sat listening to the continual tirade, getting more and more despondent. He knew that to speak up in his own defence would probably mean him ending up on some punishment detail, so he consoled himself with his thoughts instead.

OK, OK, so I've got a nice head of hair and you're jealous baldy. At least I've got some. Where's yours gone then baldy? You can laugh but at least mine hasn't fallen out, he thought to himself as 'baldy' finally got fed up with his one-man cabaret and got back to business.

Almost as soon as the electric clippers buzzed into life, Ginger realised that this was not going to be a trim up as he had hoped. Although he had more or less guessed what the outcome would be by seeing how the people ahead of him looked after their treatment, he was still taken by surprise. This was no haircut, this was a massacre as 'baldy' powered his machine up and over with obvious delight. Now it dawned on him why there was so much hair laying all over the place, as the erstwhile comedian shaved the sides and back right up until there was only a small circle of hair left on the top. Then, to add the final indignity, even that last little bit was hacked about until it was only about an inch long.

Haircut over and back outside, the boys were left to make their own way back to their mess, which was just as well because Ginger didn't feel like talking to anyone for a while. That shearing of his hair had left him feeling dehumanised and completely demoralised and he looked for the way back to his mess through misty eyes.

For the first time since he arrived he suddenly experienced the feelings of loneliness, homesickness and utter frustration overpowering him. He hadn't really minded too much for being shouted at for forgetting to clean his teeth; he hadn't minded trying on that itchy uniform and getting tangled up with the silk and lanyard, because he had to learn how to put it on unaided, but this haircut, if that's what you called it, was the final straw. He felt utterly dejected, really low. He wished he could go home.

He slouched his way back to his mess with a lump in his throat that felt as big as an orange and couldn't even bring himself to speak to his new messmates.

But so much for doing things the Navy way. Those ridiculous haircuts had achieved nothing positive but had alienated everyone from the new intake. Indeed, so much for doing things the Navy way. Using a little bit of common sense and just giving the boys a light trim up that first time, would have done wonders for morale. As haircuts were to be a two week ritual, getting shorter over the following weeks probably would have gone unnoticed and the Navy would still have got their own way. But that was not the Navy way. The Navy decreed that boys should be shorn of their hair as soon as possible and that's the way it had to be. No-one knew why or what it achieved, they just knew that was the way it had to be. It was that old chestnut over again: 'That's the Navy way and the quicker you get that into your heads, the easier things will be for you.'

It's an old saying that tells us: 'Every cloud has a silver lining,' and after a while even those rotten haircuts managed to raise a laugh or two from the boys, because now that they had all been shorn of their hair, their newly issued hats were too big and had to be changed for smaller ones.

Yes, so much for doing things the Navy way.

Having been kitted out in a brand new set of pussers clothing and sporting a brand new pussers haircut, the new boys were beginning to take on the appearance of sailors. Therefore the next step was to teach them how to act like sailors.

All they had seen so far was the inside of Jellico Two mess; the inside of the dining hall; the inside of the clothing store and the barbers shop. Now, having overcome the discomforts of sleeping in a strange bed away from home and recovered from the shock of that haircut, plus mastering where to sit and when to eat in the dining hall, their prime objective became the parade ground.

By this time the clothes they arrived in had all been parcelled up and taken to the postie's shack ready to be sent back home and they were all attired in the regulation rig-of-the-day, which was number eights, boots and gaiters.

All kit in the Navy was known by a number, ranging from number-ones, which was the best blue suit all the way to overalls, which for some reason were known simply as 'overalls' but were in fact number nines. The list continued past number nines with some items of tropical kit. But that was well into the future and the boys were not issued with tropical kit in their early days. In fact Ginger's intake was not issued with tropical kit until they had left Ganges for good. But that was well into the future and this was now. Number-ones were also a thing of the future. Their number one suit would be tailor made for them when they attained first class status, many weeks hence

Number eights was the normal work dress. It consisted of a heavy-duty light blue work shirt with a military style pocket on each breast and a pair of dark blue cotton trousers. These had to remain clean at all times and were inspected daily, very thoroughly every morning at a parade known within naval circles, as Divisions.

It was with their first Divisions that their naval training started in earnest.

Every morning straight after breakfast it was out on to the parade ground, in front of the mast—where they had first set foot in the place, off the coach that had brought them from the station—for Divisions and Divisional Officer's inspection.

The DO, as he was known, wasn't a bad sort of chap; he would walk up and down the ranks of assembled boys smiling almost continually, just stopping now and then to speak quietly to someone.

'Look lad, you have a button undone .... just do your bootlace up .... are you sure you're comfortable? You seem all bunched up ....'

Most of them soon got the hang of it. Keep all buttons buttoned and make sure your laces are tied tightly with the ends tucked out of sight. It was quite straight forward really. But there's always one. Someone who never seems to be quite up to date with everyone else. Then it became a different story, for having been told for days on end, very quietly and patiently, there came a time when enough was enough.

Then it was an aggressive snatch at an offending button, accompanied by a loud sarcastic: 'What's this then, a spare button-hole?' or: 'You here for parade drill or to do your washing lad?' Then, upon receiving confirmation that the embarrassed offender was there for parade drill like everyone else, it was:

'Well tuck your washing line inside your boot and don't let me see it again.'

The sarcasm and the ensuing embarrassment usually worked, but if it didn't have the desired effect then a few laps of the parade ground perimeter—at the double—did.

For Ginger the parade ground was a piece of cake; he knew enough about basic square bashing to get by, thanks to the army cadets and although the Navy way, as always, was slightly different, what he didn't know he was able to fake.

He was mildly surprised however, when parade drill was first mentioned because, although he hadn't given the subject very much thought before, somewhere in the back of his mind he had taken it for granted that the army did the square bashing. The army did all that marching up and down in big boots, everybody knew that, it was on the films all the time.

But the Navy? He didn't really know what the Navy did except ride about in ships and of course he knew they did that. Actually he didn't know very much about the Navy. Why he had joined up in the first place was anybodys guess, he certainly hadn't given that very much thought either. What little he did know about the Navy was gleaned from John Mills and a few others like him at the Friday night weekly picture show, in the village hall back home.

Those celluloid sailors didn't crunch about in big boots but occasionally they were required to march about a bit, on the jetty alongside their ship, when going home on leave for example. So presumably they had to have a bit of training in how to do it and this must be what this parade drill rubbish is all about. Yes, he reasoned, this must be just to teach them the basic movements so they wouldn't look out of place when they were drafted away to join a ship. Anyway he didn't mind going through it all again. It was easy and he could have a rest while the remainder of Jellicoe Two mess struggled to reach his standard.

Attention; stand at ease; left turn; right turn; about turn; quick march; slow march were all an absolute doddle, he thought to himself as he more or less wandered up and down with the rest, just going through the motions as if by remote control. It was not an entire waste of time though, because he did learn something: if you lose yourself in the middle of the centre rank you don't get noticed so much—and if you don't get noticed, you don't get shouted at.

Without realising it he was carrying on a well-respected naval tradition by weaving the first few threads toward his 'green coat'.

Only once did he get singled out.

'You're doing very well lad,' Bumble told him.

He knew he was. That army cadet training was paying off handsomely.

'But just one thing I've noticed. When you come to attention, or turn right or left, just lift your spare foot off the deck and place it down alongside your other foot. You don't have to try and hit yourself under the blinkin' chin with your knee.'

The Navy had a different way of doing everything and just this once they were right. Their way was much easier.

Very quickly the boys accepted the fact that they were there to stay and had settled down to naval routine. Whether it was deliberate policy on the Navy's part was hard to say, but they had been kept so busy throughout those first few days that thoughts of home had begun to fade and were fast becoming a distant memory.

Due to all the hustle and bustle of the hectic routine during those first few days Ginger had overlooked almost the last words his mother had said to him as he left to catch the train, what already seemed like an eternity ago.

She told him that he could send his washing home each week if he wanted to. If the truth was known she was probably quite pleased that he didn't take up her invitation. But in addition to him forgetting all about her offer and it being impractical to send dirty laundry home by post and wait for its return, there was no way on earth the Navy, as far as Ganges was concerned, would allow that to happen. Ganges kit was to be accounted for at all times and sending it all over the country by post was not part of naval tradition.

Even in those very early days they had learned that Ganges kit was to be kept clean at all times and came a close second to personal cleanliness, which was of absolute paramount importance in their estimation and very nearly a hanging offence to neglect. Clean kit was almost a religion and certainly not destined to spend days on end in transit.

So that plan, even if he had remembered, was a non-starter from the very beginning.

From the day after they were first issued with their kit the new entry boys began receiving instruction on washing clothes. Every new entry mess instructor had a line of patter which they had learned parrot fashion, or so it appeared, that they would trot out at every opportunity.

'Squeeze the soap through your socks .... always rinse with plenty of water .... never wring wool ....' etc. etc.

These phrases and more were in constant use in the Annexe, but even worse was to come, courtesy of the infamous Chalkie White. In their eagerness to turn every new recruit into a self-sufficient washing machine, the Navy in their wisdom had employed a civilian washhouse attendant. Twice a week the entire inhabitants of Jellicoe Two mess was marched to his establishment, with their laundry under their arm.

At the door the boys were handed over to Chalkie—and then it began.

First thing inside the door everyone had to strip off completely and don a slip, a kind of swimming costume with tying tapes on one side, then it was into the washhouse proper.

That place was a formidable sight for a young lad to behold. It probably wasn't that old but it had all the charm of a Victorian workhouse.

One large rectangular room stretched away to their right with sinks, side by side, all round three of the four walls and a large rinsing tank standing on the concrete floor, taking up the centre of the room. A shelf, high up, ran around the walls above the sinks. Completing the picture, on the fourth side and to their left, were racks of drying rails for hanging the wet washing on.

However formidable was the place, it would have been bearable if it was not for Chalkie White. Chalkie, as he was known by everyone, although none of the boys dared to address him by that name, was a short, mousey haired, horrible little man with a Charlie Chaplin type moustache. That man was a tartar. A strutting obnoxious little bully who loved the sound of his own voice.

The 'buzz' was that he was a former Royal Marine although it was never confirmed, not that any of the boys really cared anyway. Although the Royal Marines were known for their toughness they were never like him; compared to Chalkie White Adolph Hitler was a sister of mercy. If he had been in the marines he certainly wasn't well liked and now he had a job where he was the boss and he exercised his authority over successive intakes of new recruits with great enthusiasm

Chalkie's claim to fame was that no boys ever played about whilst in his charge. They never stepped away from where they were supposed to be; they never opened their mouth to speak for any reason and they never looked up from what they were doing without a very good cause.

Each time Ginger was in the place the routine was exactly the same and he had no reason to doubt that the boys from all the other messes were treated in the same manner as that suffered by Jellicoe Two. Once inside the door, it was undress and into a slip as quickly as possible and in complete silence. Then on a command from Chalkie—and not before—the boys would file quickly into the washhouse and stand facing a sink each. Then, when everyone was in place and Chalkie was satisfied, his washing routine would get under way.

Even so at this stage it was not a case of getting on with your washing, getting it done and getting out of that place as quickly as possible. No. Certainly not. Not while Chalkie White was in charge. Nothing was as simple and straight forward as that with that horrible little upstart running things.

Everything had to be done to a system—Chalkie's system.

Every boy had exactly the same kit to wash and the reason for that was perfectly simple: they were told what to wear, when to wear it, when to change and what to change into, so therefore it followed that what one boy had dirty, so did everyone else. This of course gave Chalkie the final lever to complete his system. Not that he needed any levers really because his awesome presence was enough to terrify even the bravest of the brave and the young lads meekly followed his egotistical orders, simply to make things as bearable as possible for themselves.

He insisted that everything had to be done in a particular sequence and his horrible high pitched voice would cackle out: 'Everyone to a sink each .... place your bundle at your feet .... socks and soap on the shelf ....'

Then on to the actual washing of the clothes: 'In the correct order .... collar and cuffs .... sleeves .... side and front,' that squawky voice would be the only sound in the place apart from the occasional 'crack' when he would slap some poor unfortunate with a strip of wood he always carried, for some petty misdemeanour like washing a sleeve when he had been instructed to wash the collar.

Whether through luck or the survival instinct, Ginger never felt the weight of that strip of wood but nevertheless he, like all the others, was totally intimidated by the ever present threat.

They were never quite sure where Chalkie was. He appeared to be able to move around at incredible speed and almost seemed to be everywhere at once. One moment he would be over the other side of the room rebuking someone for not following instructions.

'Garment to garment, lad. Garment to garment, how many times do you have to be told?'

With him way over the other side it signalled it was fairly safe to whisper out of the side of the mouth to the occupant of the next sink, but then, even before the sound of his horrible screeching voice had died away, there would be a resounding 'crack' from close by which meant that he had travelled right round the rinsing tank and someone had been caught either talking or washing something in the wrong order.

How he managed to move around so quickly and without a sound was to remain a mystery, because everyone was so intimidated by him that they were afraid to look round to see where he was; the first they knew of him looking over their shoulder was when they were screamed at for looking up or speaking without permission—or worse still, daring to wash an article of clothing in the wrong order

Even a simple operation like swishing the washed kit around in the rinsing tank was anything but simple and Chalkie could still exercise his authority.

He would take each piece, holding it first at arms length and then close up staring at it intensely, then, having passed that test, he would hold the material up to the light looking for left over stains and if that test was also satisfactory he would start picking at seams looking for minute specks of anything that could get the 'victim' dispatched back to the washing sink. By this stage most of them had been sent back to '.... do it over again', accompanied by a 'crack' from that strip of wood.

But should fortune be smiling kindly and the final test passed, Chalkie would growl quietly and almost reluctantly: 'OK lad, drying rails and don't hang about up there.'

Even at the drying rails, which pulled out of the wall on runners, they were still not safe from him. They were still in full view and woe betide anyone he thought was hanging about longer than necessary, just trying to get a couple of extra seconds respite and warmth partially hidden behind the drying kit hanging on the rails.

Quite how Chalkie came to posses so much power was a mystery. None of the boys had access to background information about him or his washhouse and how could they; to all intents and purposes their world had only started when they arrived on that coach from the station. Before then none of them had even heard of Chalkie White. All they knew about him was what they had learned at their first session together and the general consensus of opinion was that he had all the charm and friendliness of the pigswill compound.

In all probability his job was simply to keep the place clean and ensure a clean supply of rinsing water for each successive mess on their twice-weekly visits. The remainder he had undoubtedly taken upon himself to satisfy his lust for power.

He wasn't stupid though. His reign of terror never started until the instructor had left, until then he was usually quiet. As the new entry boys were afraid to say anything about him and didn't know who to complain to in any case, the chances that people in positions of authority never had any idea of what went on in Chalkies private torture chamber.

The only good thing that could be said about Chalkie White was that the boys knew his reign would be a short one. He was attached to the Annexe and the new entry intakes, which told them that they would be away and out of his reach in six weeks.

But one thing was for certain: after they had transferred to the main establishment and indeed for the rest of their lives—they would never forget Chalkie White and his rotten washing routine.

Chapter 3

Several times in the course of conversation Bumble had replied to a half-hearted complaint about the harshness of the routine in the place that 'you'll find things much better when you get over to 'The Main.'

They had all recently been whisked away from home, where they had been used to a mother to do everything for them, to the brutal contrast of the Navy where they had to do everything for themselves. This, plus all the domestic day-to-day cleaning of the establishment with the only reward that of being shouted at for not doing it properly, or not doing it quick enough or a thousand other obscure reasons that they seemed to have in reserve for an excuse to shout, had made them latch onto Bumbles words and, as time progressed, 'The Main' became a very attractive place indeed.

Quite what they expected of the main was not at all clear; each of them had formed his own opinion of how life would be different 'over there', based on what Bumble had said and as the days went by any grumble, however trivial, would be answered with the consolation that things would be different 'when we get into the main', as they all strived to assure each other that Utopia was just across the road.

They did get a foretaste of the main during their first few weeks when they were marched over for some specific purpose. But it was only a fleeting glimpse really and none of those excursions were particularly pleasant experiences for Ginger, but nevertheless those previews, which should have given them an inkling of what lay in wait for them, did nothing to dampen the enthusiasm of all concerned to get over there on a permanent basis.

It was if they had all been brain washed into thinking that the land of milk and honey was over there and was theirs for the taking.

The first of their trips over came fairly soon, when after only a couple of days Bumble announced that they would be going over to the main sickbay complex that afternoon. It was early days; they hadn't been there long and this excursion was more of an irritation than a pleasure, as the boys viewed it as a disruption in an already bewildering routine.

For some reason he said the trip over had to be in their best suit and that complicated things even further. They had only been issued with their kit a day or two before and, apart from trying it on straight after, this would be their first time of wearing a suit for a specific purpose and trying to remember how the collar, silk and lanyard went.

The entire afternoon was a bit of a non-event really as far as the boys were concerned. It was their first medical since joining, but why they had to dress up in their best suit was a bit of a mystery.

Although it was only mid May it was a hot sunny day and the number eights would have been much easier to get off and get back on again, particularly as they had to undress and get dressed again on the sick bay lawn. The heat and the complication of that collar, silk and lanyard to be arranged alone for the first time did nothing for the boys' disposition as they marched back across the road to the Annexe. For the first time since joining they were glad to see Jellicoe Two mess.

The only logical explanation for having them dress in their blue serge suit seemed to be simply to have them wear it and get used to how it felt. Ginger was not alone in knowing exactly how it felt. It was hot, itchy and downright uncomfortable.

On their next trip across the road however, the dress was to be more informal. This time the rig of the day would be sportswear, when one night just as they were getting ready for 'lights out', Bumble dropped the bombshell: 'Everyone aloft tomorrow.'

An excited murmur ran around the mess as everyone tried to talk at the same time. Well not exactly talk, because they had already learned that when Bumble said 'Silence' that was exactly what he meant and woe betide anyone who got singled out for talking after Bumble had said his goodnights and was about to turn out the lights.

'What's all that about then?' whispered Ginger to the occupant of the next bed. 'Aloft, what's that mean. What's he talking about?'

'Schhhhh, wait 'till he's gone,' was the corner of the mouth reply.

'Well goodnight lads, time to get some sleep,' Bumble said walking over toward the light switch.

He always said that, it was always those same words. But tonight no-one cared. They just wanted him to go. The atmosphere inside Jellicoe Two was electric, everyone could sense it—apart from Bumble, apparently. It was like waiting for a loud bang that you knew was coming but not quite sure when. Ginger could sense it and somehow he knew all the others could as well. The only thing that could defuse the situation was for Bumble to turn out those lights and shove off.

After what seemed like an eternity the mess descended into darkness as Bumble finally reached the switch and before his footsteps had faded as he walked along the passage to the outside door, the first blankets were thrown back and the frontrunners in the bravery stakes emerged from their beds.

It was still light outside and enough of the fading daylight came through the windows for Ginger to make out that most of the beds were now empty with their occupants converging on a huddle that was forming in the centre of the mess around one of the tables.

Bumbles footsteps had died away by this time although he couldn't have got very far and after another quick listen, just to make sure he wasn't coming back, Ginger felt brave enough to join the others.

The tension had eased a bit now that people were beginning to talk, although the atmosphere was as strong as ever. Ginger elbowed his way through the throng.

'What's going on then; what's all the fuss about; what's happening; what's all this about tomorrow?' he whispered excitedly.

'Calm down. We're going aloft tomorrow,' said a chap Ginger had never noticed before.

'I know that. Bumble just said that. What's it mean then?' he urged somewhat impatiently.

'It means that were all going to climb the mast, thicko. Don't you know nuffink,' said someone in the middle of the huddle without bothering to look up. Ginger could only see his back and it was no-one that he recognised. But at least now he had the information.

So that's what all the fuss is about, he thought rather grumpily. Climb the mast. Hardly worth getting out of bed for.

'So what's all the excitement about then?' he asked rather dejectedly and to no-one in particular. As he received no reply he pushed his way through and headed back toward his bed, leaving the rest to carry on jabbering like over excited monkeys.

By now Bumble had been completely forgotten although he had only been gone a few minutes and everyone was talking at full strength again quite oblivious to anything other than what they were going to do tomorrow. Something seemed to be in the wind although Ginger failed to fully grasp the situation. All this excitement had gone completely over his head.

As he slid back into bed he recalled that someone had mentioned climbing the mast before. That was when they were coming in on the coach from the station. He remembered someone pointing out the mast in a loud voice and saying something to the effect that they had to climb it. He hadn't paid much attention at the time. He hadn't been told anything about climbing a mast; he didn't really know what a mast was and in any case, by the time he'd looked up it was already out of sight again behind the trees. After that brief mention the mast never entered his head again.

Recalling that brief moment on the coach and coupling it with what Bumble had said and now adding the current information, He quickly put two and two together.

So we've got to climb the mast, he thought to himself. He didn't understand what all the excitement was about. A few seconds later he was asleep.

In the morning everything went on just as usual. Bumble came in shouting just like had done on previous mornings.

The boys that he had left huddled together in the centre of the mess must have got fed up and gone to bed eventually, because all beds were occupied. Well, they were until now, denoting that even the more excitable had succumbed to sleep at some stage during the night. How long they had stayed there talking didn't seem very important, the important thing right then was to get out of bed.

When Bumble came in shouting he expected everyone to leap straight out of bed.

Actually if they didn't feel like getting up right away, they could poach a few extra moments by half getting out and sitting on the side of the bed. Bumble didn't appear to notice that. Sometimes he would come in and wake everyone up and then go away again almost as quickly as he had appeared. They had soon learned that when that happened they could lay down again for a few more minutes.

It was not a good policy to hang about too long however, even if it was fairly safe to do so because that extra time in bed would put your routine all behind and when everyone else had taken their bedding apart and stacked the blankets up in the prescribed manner, you would still be racing about trying to catch up. This, of course, would make you stand out like a sore thumb and Bumble would notice. Then would come the inevitable ear bashing, at the very least.

Ginger enjoyed his few stolen moments extra in bed usually but on this particular morning everyone stirred as soon as Bumble came in and for some unknown reason, he felt obliged to follow suit.

After breakfast the morning passed quickly enough and a bit of square bashing after the ritual cleaning of the mess, took them right up to dinner time.

Dinner came and went. Then, as was usual routine, straight after dinner everyone changed into sports rig. Sports rig consisted of a coloured sports jersey, white shorts, long blue stockings and white plimsoles. That was the rig of the day every afternoon.

By this time the main topic of conversation was back to the mast again.

Ginger had failed to grasp the significance of all the excitement. He hadn't actually seen the mast and somehow he had managed to keep all thoughts of it well to the back of his mind, but now, as the time grew closer, he couldn't help but think about it. After all he would have had to be stone deaf not to have thought about it, with 'the mast' appearing in almost every sentence of everybody's conversation. He felt that he must be the only one in the entire mess that didn't know anything about 'the mast'.

Pretty soon Bumble was back. All through the morning he hadn't referred to the mast and he still gave no sign of what was to come.

'Right then lads, fall in outside.'

Just like he had said yesterday afternoon and the afternoon before that. There was nothing different at all; no tell tale signs in his voice; his face betrayed no emotion.

Ginger looked for a sign. Suddenly he felt he needed reassurance because at long last the tension was beginning to get to him. Although he didn't know why, he sensed impending doom. All the talk had finally caught up with him. The butterflies were creating havoc in his stomach.

He happened to be near the back of the mess as Bumble was ushering them out.

On a sudden impulse he ran to the back window and looked to see if he could catch sight of the mast. Looking through the glass, he could just see the top section, above the buildings. That was his first sighting of the thing. He hurried to catch up with the others as they were filing out and that momentary glimpse made him feel at lot easier. It didn't look too bad, in fact it looked fairly easy and by the time he arrived outside the mess with the others, most of his newly acquired tension had subsided.

The routine was familiar by now and the boys quickly formed themselves into three ranks, facing their mess. Sometimes someone would get it wrong then it would be a loud snappy: 'Come on then, you know the routine. Tallest on the flanks, shortest in the centre.'

But this time everything went like clockwork and by the time Bumble gave them his full attention, he was faced by three smart ranks of boys, standing properly at ease, tallest on the flanks, shortest in the centre and there was no need for him to say anything.

In fact he didn't say anything and as the boys turned right and wheeled left out of the gate, under the orders of their instructor boy, the atmosphere was quite relaxed. The whole class seemed to take on an air of happiness as they marched along the road toward the main gate of the main establishment. It was like the atmosphere of a school outing, even the instructor boy seemed quite happy; he didn't appear to notice the amount of chattering that was going on.

Apparently Ginger was the only one not convinced that this afternoon jaunt was as good as an afternoon off.

Although most of the tension that he had felt earlier had left him by this time, he still had reservations about the whole thing. Somewhere in the back of his mind was a niggling doubt. He didn't know why exactly but that doubt just kept gnawing away. As it was to turn out he was right to have those doubts...

Suddenly everything went quiet as the marching feet left the unmade road and joined the public road that led to the main gate. The sudden, indeed abrupt, transition from gravel to tarmac brought an instant response from the boys and as plimsoled feet made contact with the flat hard surface and the crunching noise stopped, so did the talking. It was as if it was all right to talk while the gravel disguised the noise but the tarmac was a different matter. Plimsoles made very little noise and none of them felt brave enough to speak now that every word could be heard.

Directly in front they could see the main establishment entrance gate. Each step took them closer and with each step they took in more detail. It was a long stretch of road leading up to the gate and that gave them a certain amount of time to take in their surroundings.

To their left was a long, new looking building. It was obviously a cookhouse because of the smell of cooking coming from that direction and, in any case, there was a couple of blokes standing near an open door wearing white cooks uniform.

In fact it was the dining hall and galley for the main establishment.

It was an impressive building and something of a Navy showpiece, but the boys hardly noticed. By this stage, their eyes were straight ahead mesmerised by that gate and what lay beyond.

The arms swung just that little bit higher and the step was that little bit brisker as they passed between the two old fashioned cannons that were standing sentinel and entered through the double iron gates.

The guardroom was directly to the left as they passed in front of it. At the end of the guardroom they wheeled left and as they turned the corner of the building, they got their first sight of the mast, to their right.

A few paces straight ahead brought them to the edge of the parade ground. Just on to the parade ground, then a right wheel had them heading for the mast. They were halted right in front of the mast and almost under the edge of the safety net. It was the first time they had been this way although they must have passed close by on their way to the sick bay a few days before.

It was the first time Ginger had seen the entire thing. Actually he still couldn't see the whole mast because it was so high and they were right underneath it. They could only see the top by leaning back and turning their heads right up, skywards.

'Into line, right turn,' that was the first time Bumble had spoken since leaving Jellicoe Two mess.

They were now standing in three ranks in front of and facing the mast.

Between them and the mast, right on the edge of the parade ground, was an old sailing ships cannon. Ginger only knew what it was because he had seen similar things at the pictures. He couldn't help looking at it, it was right in front of him, he was in the centre rank but he could see between the boys directly in front of him.

A cannon stood in front of and either side of the mast, just under the edge of the safety net. They were not like the ones outside the main gate, they were the larger army type ones with the big spoked wheels, very much like the guns used in the field gun displays, although he didn't know that. These ones were much smaller, typical old sailing ships armament—although he didn't know that either.

He took in every detail of those small guns in their wooden carriages, with their small wooden wheels. The little touch hole at the back for lighting the charge; the little wedges for holding the wheels on .... He didn't appreciate what he was looking at, really he didn't really care. In all probability his interest was subconsciously triggered to keep his thoughts away from the mast.

Anyway they were so close they couldn't see the mast properly. Bumble didn't want them straining about, leaning all over the place, trying to look up to see the top. All they could see clearly was the bottom of the rigging and the safety net.

'Right then lads, pay attention. This is the mast. Every boy has to do a mast test as part of his training. Don't worry, it's not as bad as it looks.'

That was Bumble addressing his charges as he strode up and down in front of the assembled boys.

'When the officer comes, it will be up one side onto the platform, round and up to the second platform and back down the other side. Don't worry it's not so bad: up, over and down the other side. A piece of cake. Right then, pay attention. We'll march round to the far side of the rigging and stand by for orders to man the mast.'

As they turned left into file and marched on leaving the mast to their right, Ginger felt pleased that he was toward the back. But as they moved into position, tragedy struck.

'Class halt,' shouted Bumble—and then disaster.

'ABOUT TURN.'

They were now facing the rigging in three files. By turning about it had put him near the front. Only the fact that he wasn't the tallest saved him from being in the very front.

The rigging they had to climb was a kind of vertical rope net with mesh of about nine inches square. It looked easy enough and in any case someone else was going first. He still felt uneasy about the whole thing but at the same time he couldn't think why. It looked simple enough and there were plenty of hand-holds.

'There's nothing to worry about,' Bumble was assuring them. 'Just do exactly as you're told and everything will be just fine. You will approach the rigging four abreast and on the command you will begin to climb. Just like I've told you; up one side and down the other.'

By this time an officer had arrived and an Instructor Boy pushed past and climbed up.

'Right then. Stand by. First four, man the rigging.'

That was the order to stand at the bottom of the net, holding it with both hands and one foot on the bottom mesh.

Now things were under way. 'First four aloft.'

The first four started to climb the net and when they were just out of reach—'Next four man the rigging.' So it went on. 'Next four aloft. Next four man the rigging.' Ginger's fear had vanished; it looked easy enough. Being a country boy he had climbed trees back home with his school chums and, if anything this was easier. There was a big net to hold on to and plenty of footholds. It was more or less like climbing a rope ladder.

He was in the third wave and, as if by some kind of magic considering his early nerves, all his tension and fear had gone.

'Next four man the rigging.'

That was his cue. He stepped forward and grabbed the rope rigging, eager to be getting on with it.

The previous four were out of reach now and Bumbles voice rang out again.

'Next four aloft.'

He was looking forward to this now and he was away up the rigging like a monkey with its tail on fire.

If only he had known.

The first platform—the big one—was about fifty feet or so from the ground. He hadn't looked up, or at least if he had he hadn't taken in what he saw. His only interest was in the next handhold in front of him as he scrambled ever upward.

Naturally the rigging was anchored to the ground at the bottom end and the top was secured firmly to the platform, but it wasn't pulled tight enough to make it rigid. All those boys climbing on it at the same time was making the whole section swing and bounce about. Ginger hadn't taken this into account and the first he was aware of it was when he missed a handhold.

Suddenly the net wasn't where he expected it to be when he grabbed for a new grip and he was left pawing the air. He missed it with his hand completely as he misjudged the bounce and this made him swing crazily. One foot that was already on its way to the next step also missed its mark and this made him swing and bounce about all over the place, mainly supported by just one hand, he found himself shaken about until he had turned right round and his back was to the net. Just for a second he had visions of being stranded there, hanging helpless, but the action of the net bounced him round and back into position again, he made sure this time by catching hold with both hands.

The net was swinging about from side to side and also bouncing in toward the mast quite considerably as he tried to steady his reeling senses. Now he knew why those niggling doubts had pestered him all the way over.

One thing he hadn't bargained for suddenly hit him like a thunderbolt—he was incredibly afraid of heights.

He had no inkling before. He'd climbed those trees back home like the rest of them without a second thought. He had never had reason to suspect anything like this and swaying about forty feet above the ground was not the best time to find out.

Strangely his acrobatics took no time at all and although it felt like an eternity, swinging about like a rag doll in the breeze, the boys following didn't even have to check their pace. In fact he hardly faltered in his own upward momentum. The rigging tossed him back into his climbing position and despite the almost overpowering dizzy, sickening feeling, instinct carried him on.

The next ten steps or so were climbed entirely by remote control, with no knowledge of where he was or what he was doing, until his head met the rigging that went round the Devil's Elbow. This brought him back to reality because he had to find his way round the edge of that net and climb up through the hole in the main platform.

'Come on, come on, you're not up here to admire the view.'

That was the Instructor Boy stationed on the main platform. He was there to make sure everybody got up through the hole and round onto the next section of the rigging for the remainder of their journey.

'Come on then, come ....', his voice trailed away. He must have realised that the look on Ginger's face was a look of sheer terror.

'OK, OK, you're doing fine. Don't look down. You're OK.'

'I can't .... I can't do it,' He had never been so high before.

'Course you can, you've done the hard bit,' as he spoke, the Instructor Boy was edging forward until Ginger had nowhere to go but round the edge of the rigging.

'Don't look down. Look in front of you. Concentrate on what you're doing.' Ginger had his full attention. That Instructor Boy was right there with him.

He searched for his first foothold without daring to look for it. He was terrified, his legs were shaking and he felt sick. He wanted to insist that he just couldn't do it, but that Instructor Boy wasn't giving him enough time to think, let alone speak. All the time he was trying to object he was being forced back until, without fully realising it, he was on the rigging and continuing on his way aloft.

This time the mesh in the rigging was smaller and as he got closer to the second platform it got so small there was hardly enough room to put his feet in. He was almost beside himself with fear but at the same time he was more afraid of the humiliation and ridicule of everyone knowing than of the mast itself. Somehow he struggled on.

The second platform, or as Bumble had called it—the half moon, was about 110 feet above the ground. It was only about eight feet across and a lot less in width and very small compared to the main platform, some fifty odd feet below. It was of metal construction and designed a bit like a half circular metal grating and the grating effect made it easier for extra handholds.

Another Instructor Boy was standing on the half moon, with his back to the mast.

As his eyes came level with the grating, Ginger caught sight of the Instructor Boy's legs. He'd been so preoccupied on the other platform that he hadn't noticed what the other one was wearing but this one was still wearing his blue suit, he hadn't changed into sports rig.

Those legs were a welcome sight because at this stage the rigging was so narrow that it was single file up and over the half moon and that meant, for a while at least, he was completely alone. Those legs certainly were a welcome sight and as soon as he was high enough, he made a grab for them and held on as if his life depended upon it, which it probably did.

'I can't make it. I can't. I can't,' he mumbled very embarrassed but nevertheless speaking the truth.

'You're OK. I'll help you,' said the blue suit.

Ginger didn't know who this chap was; he didn't look at his face, he was too busy hanging on.

'You've done it. Just across here and down the other side. It's easy now, you're on your way down and finish. Come on. Stand up.'

Ginger accepted the offered hand and slowly hauled himself up, reluctantly releasing his grip on those legs.

'That's right, pass across in front of me,' that Instructor Boy had a reassuring voice and he found himself doing exactly as he was told.

Over a hundred feet up in the air and he was standing up. The mast swayed, or rather jerked, just a bit but luckily there was no wind whatsoever. He didn't feel brave enough to look around though and he kept his eyes firmly fixed on the Instructor Boy's hand.

'You're OK. Don't look down, Just feel for the net with your foot,' the blue suit could probably sense the fear.

His foot made contact with the down side rigging and he leaned slowly forward until his free hand could grasp a hold on the metal. He still had a firm hold of the Instructor Boy with his other hand, a grip he was not ready to relinquish until he had backed over the edge of the half moon and had both feet and his free hand securely on the rigging.

The holds were small and awkward to force his feet into but he didn't mind, he was on his way down and those holds were getting bigger all the time. He descended that section in record time. It didn't appear to take anything like as long as it did going up the other side. Going down was easier and he was speeded on by the thought that he would soon be on the ground again.

When he reached the main platform he actually ran across to the hole in his eagerness to get down the last section—a different story from the one on the way up.

Through the hole and round the devils elbow rigging without a moments hesitation; his little climbing excursion had given him a bit of temporary confidence, particularly as he knew each step took him one step nearer the ground.

With his newly found bravery he was soon back on *terra firma*. As his feet touched the ground his knees buckled for a split second, but he didn't care, he'd made it down safely.

He stood facing the rigging just like he had started off on the other side and, still with his hands on the net, he took a deep breath and an extra second to try and control his shaking.

There was just one more formality to complete the afternoons exercise: doubling round to the officer and standing to attention PT style, with fingers outstretched fully extended by the sides, giving your name and reporting: 'Returning from aloft, sir,' did the trick.

That was the easiest bit of the whole afternoon and when it was Ginger's turn he knew it signalled an end to the whole ordeal. He wasn't sure what they had achieved by climbing the mast but at least he had done it.

Chapter 4

The 'buzz' went round: 'There's a boxing tournament on Wednesday and everyone has to box in it.'

This was yet another of those ridiculous naval traditions. It was as if a flap falls over the brain with the words 'All New Entrants Must Box' written on it and although no-one really knew why 'that's how it's always been and that's the way it is.'

There were no exceptions. Boxing had been decreed and boxing there would be. It didn't matter a toss if you had been a schoolboy champion or had never seen a pair of gloves close up before, the entire intake, immaterial of athletic status or boxing ability, was summoned to appear and everyone had to don the gloves.

Way back in the mists of time boxing had come to the fore and that's where it had stayed ever since. No-one really knew why; no-one questioned it.

They didn't care if you could play football or tiddlywinks. They didn't care if you could drive a car or fly a 'plane. No-one cared if you practiced some form of martial art, like judo or something, which could have conceivably have been of some use later on.

At this stage no-one even cared if you could swim, which for naval personnel one would have thought would have been high on their list of priorities.

No, the only thing on anyone's mind was that boxing and everyone must box.

Being new entries the boys were all well documented with every conceivable detail about them being down on paper, so the matchmakers job was simplicity itself.

All he had to do was match pairs of boys of the same weight together, with no thought to their physical ability or their boxing attributes. In fact he never ever met the boys individually, to him they were just names and weights to be paired together. So the first time any of them knew who their opponent was to be, or what time their bout would take place, was when the entire list was nailed up outside Beatty One mess.

Although Ginger wasn't looking forward to the boxing, he wasn't particularly worried about it either because he had done a bit with the army cadets back home. Well, to be more precise, he'd had the gloves on a few times in their meeting hut but that certainly wasn't ABA stuff, it was just a muck about with his school mates. They didn't have a ring or any fancy boxing kit or anything like that, they just knocked each other round the hut for a few minutes until someone suggested a cup of tea. That was the extent of his boxing experience so he couldn't call himself an accomplished boxer, but nevertheless he'd had the gloves on and that gave him a little bit of confidence.

By contrast, Humph, the boy who had the next bed, was a bit of a boxing champion and eventually when their Ganges time was over, Humph wanted to be a PTI. Humph wasn't a know-all like some of them but he knew boxing and could talk with authority on the subject. Having joined straight from Holbrook sea training school he was accustomed to being away from home and was not troubled by the nerves and uncertainties that the rest of them shared in common. That, plus his boxing knowledge, gave him an air of confidence.

Unfortunately talking to Humph about boxing had the reverse effect on Ginger and instead of giving him a more positive attitude, he was beginning to have serious doubts about his own fistic ability and those doubts had started to eat away at what little confidence he had to start with.

So, as soon as that list went up, he was quickly on the scene to check up on who his opponent was to be.

Checking the notice board he found that he was matched against a boy called Bright. Bright was not from Jellicoe Two and Ginger made it his business to look him over. He just wanted to size him up and a few discreet enquiries soon had him sighted. Bright turned out to be a pale, not very healthy looking, nervous fair haired chap and a few more discreet enquiries revealed that he had never boxed before and the forthcoming tournament had turned him into a bundle of nerves.

This information gave Ginger some of his recently lost confidence back, the confidence that Humph had unwittingly undermined. But just the same, when he joined the audience prior to his turn in the ring, he sat next to Humph for a bit of moral support.

The boxing venue was tucked in behind the dining hall at the far end of the parade ground and by the time he arrived the show was well under way.

In the middle of the floor was the ring, with the PT officer and a couple of PTIs from the main sitting at ringside. The officer was the timekeeper.

He had a four-inch shell case hanging upside down for a bell. It sounded more like a Chinese gong when he hit it but a bell it was and many an unwilling contestant was very relieved to hear it 'bong' at the end of their three rounds.

The two PTIs were busy with pencil and pad, probably keeping score or looking for likely talent to join the base boxing team. The picture was completed by two more PTIs who were on the ring apron, acting as seconds— and, of course, the contestants who were marched up two at a time to perform their three round 'duty'. The only spectators were the contestants awaiting their turn in the ring. All boys had to report twenty minutes before their scheduled bout time and that ensured a reasonable sized audience to clap and cheer, without knowing, or caring, why.

Why they insisted on going through this ritual every six weeks, with every successive intake was a mystery because no-one appeared to be very interested, certainly not the vast majority of contestants anyway.

It was repetitious and boring, next two; stand up; sit down; three rounds; next two

Then it was Ginger's turn.

'Sit on the stool lad, while I put your gloves on.'

He obediently sat down and held out his hands for the cornerman to push the gloves on and lace them up. He didn't really know much about competition boxing but he reflected on the lack of bandages for the hands; no gum shield; no head guard, in fact no form of protection at all. But he consoled himself with the knowledge that all the other contestants were the same.

'In the blue corner, Boy Bright,' droned the impersonal voice of one of the 'pad and pencil' PTIs, without bothering to look up from his pad to see if it was Bright, or indeed, if anyone was there at all. Bright stood up, nervously took the required one pace forward and self consciously stood to attention.

Good God, don't you look a sight, Ginger thought to himself, as Bright's pathetic figure stood alone diagonally across the ring. He was wearing rig-of-the-day sportswear, consisting of a far too big pair of white tropical shorts that reached down to his knees, with the too large waistband all bunched up at mid-chest level. His skinny little arms protruded out from a singlet type vest and hung limply by his sides, as if weighed down by what appeared enormous boxing gloves.

As Bright stepped back and sat down again, the thought crossed Ginger's mind that he looked just as bad.

Then it was his turn.

As his name was called his second gave him a shove and he stumbled forward, stood to attention, took one step backwards and sat down again. At the same time thinking how stupid it was trying to stand to attention in a boxing ring whilst wearing plimsoles.

Bong went the gong.

'Round One.'

Here we go. Humph was watching so he was determined to make a good show. Keep sticking out the left hand; he knew how to do that and just feint occasionally with a right cross or uppercut to keep Bright at arms length.

That's basic stuff, but the round seemed to go on a lot longer than when the previous pair where in there.

He had never been a full three minutes before; it seemed to go on for an eternity and his arms ached something awful.

Bong went the gong.

Well that was the first round over at last. Three minutes seemed more like an hour. As the cornerman dragged him down onto the stool his mind was full of activity. I've not been hurt .... in fact I don't think I let him lay a glove on me .... keep this up and I've waltzed it.

Bong. 'Round Two.'

Here we go again. He was off his stool and eager to be getting on with it. Humph was out there somewhere watching so a bit more dancing this time, just to put a bit of polish on the performance.

'Stop boxing.'

That was the PT officer from outside the ring. There wasn't a referee inside the ring.

'Come over here, the pair of you.'

Ginger and Bright walked to the ropes above where the PT officer was sitting. During the interval he had forgotten how much his arms ached and this unexpected interlude gave him a chance to relax for a few extra seconds.

'What's the matter with you two. This is supposed to be a boxing match. We are already half way through the second round and neither of you has landed a blow yet. You are allowed to hit each other.'

Ginger felt sure the man was calling them over so he could congratulate him on a fine performance but instead here they were being ridiculed by this idiot and with Humph watching.

In the entire course of history there was never a thirty second silence that took so long to pass. The place was in total silence. They both stood looking down at the PT officer, not sure of what to do next.

It was him that broke the silence.

'Right, centre of the ring. Continue boxing and let's see more action this time!'

Two shame faced boys continued to paw the air but this time with a bit more conviction, until the end of the round.

During the second interval Ginger's second said: 'If you don't shape up lad, you're going to blow it. This third round is your last chance to catch the judge's eye if you want to win through to the next leg. So let's see lots more action this time.'

The next leg. He hadn't given a thought to any more fights. He didn't want any more rotten boxing. This was quite enough thank you. Let those that like it get on with it; he'd done his bit. That officer said that they hadn't hit each other enough but he ached all over. If that's what it feels like when you haven't been hit enough, what's it feel like when you get a bit of a beating? He just hoped Humph hadn't been paying attention. Yes thank you. He'd had enough of that; he certainly didn't want any more.

Poor old Bright got the decision—and progressed into the next leg, while Ginger added a few more threads toward his green coat.

The remainder of the boxing, up to and including the finals would be undertaken at a later stage after they had moved over to the main on a permanent basis. How Bright fared in the following legs wasn't of interest, they never saw each other again.

Sports featured prominently in the lives of all boys over in the main. Sports of all kinds were played every afternoon over there, the Annexe boys could usually hear the cheering.

Although the rig of the day was sportswear every afternoon, the new boys didn't get to indulge in sport very often. Of course in those first few weeks they didn't realise what they were missing, all they knew was what Bumble wanted them to know. Bumble would never impart more information than was necessary to get them through the immediate future.

They would change after dinner every day just because that was what was decreed. Very often there was no reason at all—apart from it being the Navy way. An announcement would cackle out over the Tannoy system: 'All boys to change. Rig of the day, sportswear.'

That would be the only warning and if Bumble should come back after dinner and find some poor unfortunate that hadn't changed—well, look out for high jinks. No-one ever lagged behind twice.

There had been a few afternoons when their activities could loosely come under the heading of sports, like when they climbed the mast and the boxing. But as a general rule their first few weeks were not particularly sports orientated, despite wearing sports rig every afternoon.

A few times there had been extra marching and parade drill in the afternoons, for those a bit slow to catch on. But even that would be carried out in sports gear and plimsoles.

It didn't happen very often and usually didn't involve many people but nevertheless the rig of the day was sports gear despite that fact there was no sport to get involved with.

Ginger was fortunate that he'd had the benefit of the army cadets training, such as it was, before he had joined up. It was pretty basic stuff and he hadn't really paid that much attention but enough of it had sunk in for him to coast through the Annexe training without raising a sweat, so he never had to perform any of that extra afternoon instruction. That meant that on the odd afternoon when there wasn't organised activities, or when Bumble was occupied with trying to help a small group out on the parade ground, he had a free period.

It wasn't a free period really. But if you had enough sense to keep out of the way as best you could, you could sometimes wander about until tea time with nothing to do. Another good trick was to leave a couple of bits of kit, without having the name sewn in with the red silk. Something that wouldn't be immediately noticed, like a blue suit and then if you did get caught you could explain that you were just looking for a bit of the red silk, to finish off your last bit of sewing. More threads toward his 'green coat.'

On one such 'free period' he really touched lucky.

He was just skiving out of Jellicoe Two when, at the door he stopped to have his usual cautionary look round, to ensure the coast was clear, when he saw a boy carrying some cricket gear.

This was something new. No-one had ever mentioned cricket and, as far as he was aware, cricket had not been played in the Annexe before, certainly not during his intake. This looked like a golden opportunity to look busy without actually doing anything, so he enquired what was going on.

'We've got a game of cricket organised for behind the sick bay,' the boy explained.

Ginger's face lit up. 'I'll help you carry the gear if you like,' he volunteered.

He walked forward briskly and before the boy could accept his offer—or object for that matter, he had grabbed an armful of pads from him and was following along.

This was perfect. If Bumble or anyone else saw him now he would be safe. He was helping with the cricket.

The boy led the way around the end of the sick bay and on to a small patch of grass directly behind the Divisional Office. This was better still. The small enclosure was completely out of sight. He hadn't noticed it there before so the chances were that it wasn't used very often and therefore unlikely that anyone would look for him there.

The cricket organiser was one of the sick berth attendants. He vaguely remembered him from when they got some of their never ending succession of jabs.

'Come on Ginger, put those pads down and come over here with this team,' he said. Better and better; he had completely accepted him. He hadn't noticed that he sent one boy to get the gear and two had come back. Ginger quickly complied. He didn't want to rock the boat; he didn't want to do anything that would get him singled out or remembered especially.

He hadn't reckoned on playing. He thought he would just watch and pretend to be interested. At least he was out of sight round there.

But this was even better. This was great. If he was playing his afternoon was safe.

As an added bonus Ginger liked this chap. This was the first person—other than the boys of course, who didn't want you to stand to attention every time he spoke. He seemed human, just like a normal person. He didn't shout or give orders. He didn't expect to be called sir. He addressed the boys as equals and very quickly the boys cottoned on. Without becoming over familiar, they treated him the same.

A wonderful relaxed atmosphere soon developed, thanks to that man. Ginger and his newly found team mates were enjoying a splendid informal afternoon although he had no business being there in the first place. For a couple of glorious hours the Navy was completely forgotten.

He wasn't much of a cricket player, his game was football. He was pretty hot stuff with a football, or at least he thought so. But today, a brilliantly hot sunny day, he had landed on his feet for once and he was enjoying the game.

His team did the bowling and fielding first and that was just great. He didn't want to get too involved with batting and being centre of attention.

There's always front runners anyway, the ones that want to do everything and be everywhere and he was quite happy to let them get on with it. As they were sorting out who would do the bowling, who would be wicketkeeper, who would be in the slips, he was trying his best not to get picked. That green coat was coming along nicely.

All the time they were squabbling with each other over who was to do what and competing for particular positions, he was edging further backward, until at last all the important positions were taken and he could lose himself out on the boundary, in a place where he guessed the ball wouldn't get hit very often. He did have the presence of mind however, to position himself away from the gap at the end of the sick bay, where they had come in—just in case someone should come looking for him.

He was almost a spectator anyway and that was all he had ever planned on being.

From his position on the outfield he could survey the whole scene and a little cheer, or a bit of clapping occasionally when the others did so, ensured that he was still part of the game.

With very little to do as far as participation in the game was concerned, apart from picking up the odd loose ball that came his way and throwing it back, he had plenty of time to study the other individuals. He didn't know any of them or where they were from, but more to the point none of them had singled him out as an interloper.

Watching that SBA, who was acting as umpire, team manager for both teams and coach, it suddenly dawned why he seemed familiar. Ginger knew that he was one of the medical staff and now that he had a bit of time to think, the penny dropped.

It was a couple of days previously. They were queuing up outside the sick bay waiting for yet another opportunity to perform as a pin cushion for the medical branch darts team, when Jasper voiced his concern over the prospect of another sore arm. Jasper was a very small lad. The smallest one in Jellicoe Two by a long way.

Some quick witted individual saw a heaven sent opportunity for a bit of a leg pull. 'Have you seen the size of the needles they're using this time?' he cracked.

Puck, who was nearby in the queue, cottoned on straight away. A look at poor little Jaspers face told them they had his full attention; he was as white as a sheet.

'Yeh,' said Puck, picking up on the theme of the joke. 'I've got a mate over in the main and he told me that this is the big jab. Everybody gets one; he warned me about it. He said the needle goes right through your arm.'

Jasper didn't want to hear any more, he couldn't anyway—he was on the ground fast asleep. He had fainted.

That's where Ginger had seen that SBA before. It was him that had come running out of the sick bay to help Jasper to his feet and assure him that needles did no such thing and that he would be all right. He was a nice bloke, a genuine sort of chap and most unusual for Ganges. Although he had been very busy that afternoon he had seen Jasper collapse and had immediately come to his aid. He'd messed up a good joke, but with hindsight he had done the right thing. The joke was a bit nasty. Jasper hadn't found it in the least amusing.

Being so small Jasper had been in the centre of quite a bit of merriment, one way or another. It wasn't a case of him being picked on because of his size. Quite the contrary. He was a friendly young lad and he had a sharp line in witty repartee usually—except when he was worrying about long needles of course. He also had a big grin that was infectious and endeared him to everyone.

The first day in the place Jasper had everyone in fits of laughter when, quite innocently, he asked: 'I wonder how long it will be before I'm an admiral?'

Then, when they were issued with their kit, he was in the spotlight again. Being so small his hat was also very small, the smallest size they had in fact. This brought forth roars of laughter when some of the biggest boys paraded up and down Jellicoe Two 'modelling' Jaspers tiny hat.

Jasper must have been fractionally taller that the Navy's minimum height requirement.

Chapter 5

Having joined the Navy it seemed reasonable that one would be expected to get used to water. Up until now no-one had really given it very much thought. In those early days there was always something to do, almost every moment of the day and thinking wasn't part of it; thinking wasn't something they were encouraged to do, particularly during those early days in the Annexe.

They were told what to do and when to do it—and to follow that line without thinking or question. Or, in other words, follow orders, don't question them.

Although water would play an important part in their young lives as they progressed through their service careers, not many of them, if any, realised that fact. The majority of them had forgotten why they had joined up and were quite prepared to reverse that process at a moments notice. This was not a bit like they expected the Navy to be and most of them were quite prepared to forget the whole thing and go back home.

Water would certainly play a significant role one way or another, in all sailors lives and from the very beginning Ganges boys were thrown in at the deep end, metaphorically speaking. Apparently the Navy had not heard of doing things in easy stages. 'Gradually' was not a word they had in their vocabulary.

Having recovered from the shock of meeting Chalkie White and his washhouse for the first time and having managed, to some degree, to build up some kind of mental resistance to his tyrannical ego, the Navy now thought it time to inflict another form of water torture on the poor unfortunates and this would take the form of a swimming test.

It had been decreed, somewhere back long ago, that all boys should pass a standard swimming test and to this end, their introduction to the swimming bath over in the main, was undertaken while they were still attached to the Annexe, during their first few weeks.

The object of the exercise was just to ascertain who could already swim and who couldn't. It would have been quite simple to ask for anyone that couldn't swim to say so. But no, that would have been far too easy; that certainly was not the Navy way of doing things. The Navy didn't do anything the straight forward easy way if there was the possibility of complicating things out of all proportion.

So, one afternoon the whole of Jellicoe Two mess was marched over to the main establishment swimming bath, to take the prescribed swimming test. At this stage no-one had even mentioned the possibility that some of them might not be able to swim.

It was a lovely hot sunny day and Ginger felt perfectly at ease as they entered the changing room in front of the pool. He couldn't swim but that was a minor point and didn't bother him at this stage. He was enjoying a trip out away from the Annexe and all the hustle and bustle of Navy nozzers routine.

The fears, uncertainties and butterflies that had tormented him on their last trip over, when they had to climb the mast, was way behind him now. This time he was calm and collected and enjoying to what amounted to an afternoon off—he was beginning to settle down at last. Maybe this was the first stage of him becoming a blase old hand.

The trip was made in sports rig this time and that was much easier to get off.

'Right then lads, strip off as quickly as possible and then we'll go through the foot bath in front of you and into the swimming pool .'

The boys obediently followed Bumbles instructions and, completely naked, they made their way through to the poolside where they congregated very self-consciously in a huddle at the shallow end.

Inside they were met by the PTIs who were waiting to take them through the swimming test.

'Right then, come on fall in, in three ranks along here.'

In their naked state the boys were slow to respond and shuffled forward slowly, shoulders hunched and arms crossed in front of their body, embarrassed to be naked in front of strangers.

'Come on, come on, we haven't got all day,' screamed the PTI in charge. 'Stand up straight, put your hands at your sides properly. What's the matter with you—we've all got one.'

That little crack helped to ease the tension caused by embarrassment and made the boys feel a bit more comfortable. After all they were men now and in there, they were all men together.

'Good God, lad, we haven't all got one like that.'

Those few words did the trick. Most of them laughed out loud, which in turn encouraged even more laughter until nearly everyone in the place was laughing. Even the very timid managed a snigger behind their hands and the embarrassment and tension was gone.

Little did they know that routine, with almost those very words, had been used by PTIs in naval swimming baths in every barracks in the country for the past thirty years. Apparently it always worked and now the latest recruits to receive the treatment were ready for the business in hand, with all the stiff awkwardness and shyness banished for ever.

The remainder of the session was easy.

'Any non-swimmers?'

Ginger stepped forward, he couldn't swim a stroke. A few others also stepped forward.

'OK non-swimmers, go and sit in the pens behind you,' said one of the PTIs.

The swimming pool was a lovely modern place and 'the pens' were a small walled off spectator area, at the shallow end. As the non-swimmers made their way to the pens the remainder were putting on duck suits—old fashioned white tropical uniforms made of canvas—ready to take the test.

The swimming test consisted of jumping in at the shallow end and swimming up to the far end and back again. Then, without touching the sides or bottom, about three quarters of the way back again where the swimmer had to float about for a further three minutes, still wearing the suit and without touching the sides.

It didn't look too difficult and all those that took part managed to pass without too much trouble. Ginger sat watching proceedings with interest, little realising that he would be required to do the same in the not too distant future.

As soon as the last batch of swimmers finished their test, they all trooped back into the changing room to get dressed. Ginger felt good. He'd had a nice afternoon off and hadn't had to do a thing. He didn't even get wet, apart from his feet when he went through the foot-bath and they had dried while he had been sitting in the pens. As he pulled on his long stockings and tied his plimsoles he reflected on what a lovely day it was; the sun was shining and he had enjoyed an afternoon out.

He didn't know what lay in store for him at a later date courtesy of the Backward Swimmers Class, which would have to be undertaken in his spare time until he could pass that test. But that was still to come, no-one had mentioned that, he had no idea, in any case he wasn't bothered. He was at peace with the world and he'd had a lovely afternoon.

A lovely afternoon was what was planned for their next trip across to the main, although things don't always work out the way they are planned.

This time it would be an official 'ceremonial' afternoon. They were invited to watch the QBR—Queens Birthday Review. The QBR was a big parade over in the main establishment that all of Ganges had been practising for weeks. Brass Hats, Big Wigs and local dignitaries were invited every year, so rumour had it; each year it was the biggest and best service display for miles and they came in droves.

Last year, they said, was an extra special parade and an historic occasion, because the King had just died and Queen Elizabeth the Second had taken over for the first time.

The Queen decreed that June the fifth was to be her Official Birthday and it was last year, but this time, for reasons best known to themselves, the QBR was held on June 11.

Although the new boys were invited to witness the review, it was not the kind of invitation that could be declined, it was not an invitation really, at all. The boys received their first taste of a service 'invitation' and although there was no way out of it, their recruitment had landed on their feet for once; just for once something had worked in their favour.

They had only been in the place for about four weeks and therefore hadn't had enough time to train for the big occasion. Without realising it and without lifting a finger in their own defence, they had managed to avoid the biggest parade of the Ganges year.

However, having no part to play didn't mean they were free to do as they wished. They had been 'invited' to attend as spectators. This, they were to learn, was nearly as bad as taking part. Bumble made them dress in their best uniform and they were inspected as thoroughly as if they were the central characters although they had no part to play.

What did play a big part was the weather.

Ever since their first day in early May, the weather had been lovely, weather more usually associated with August than early June. They'd had lovely warm sunny weather every day since joining up, but on the day designated for QBR it poured down.

At breakfast time it was pouring; at nine it was pouring; at 1015 it was decided to put the start time back in the hope that the rain might stop, but at 1130, when they finally got under way it was still pouring down.

The new recruits were lucky in that they were allowed to wear oilskins over their best suits and although the Blanco still ran down their necks, after parting company with their hats, they were much better off than the people in the review. They had no coats and pretty quickly they were soaked to the skin and covered in white Blanco, which ran from hats, belts and gaiters and made a lovely mess on blue uniforms.

The 'buzz' was that it never rained on KBR—Kings Birthday Review— and someone remembered that it hadn't rained on this day for the past 28 years. But the second Queens Birthday Review made up for all those dry parades. It rained continuously all day.

Ginger didn't really know what was going on. He wasn't into big parades, although this one, which took place on the playing fields behind Nelson Hall, was certainly something. It was the biggest parade he had ever seen. The band and the guard put on a good show and were as smart as they could be, bearing in mind they were soaking wet, covered in Blanco and quite possibly downright miserable. The 21 gun salute followed by 'Three Cheers for Her Majesty' was very impressive; it was a stirring experience all right, although a bit uncomfortable in the wet.

Despite not knowing, or caring, who they were, he felt sorry for some of the families that had come to watch. He wondered how they could possibly dry off.

The lads weren't too bad really, they had Bumble to fuss over them and show them the best way to clean up. In any case their oilskins saved them a lot of bother and quite quickly they were back to normal again, with their first ever QBR, impressive as it was, almost forgotten by tea time.

During all the hassle of drying off their wet clothes and trying to remove Blanco from everywhere, Ginger noticed one young lad come into the mess long after the rest of them had been back. They called him Puck although he didn't know him very well.

Puck looked perfectly clean and dry and this caught Ginger's eye.

'How come you're not wet like the rest of us then, mate?' he asked as Puck walked by. He couldn't figure out how Puck had managed to stay so dry.

Ginger recalled that Puck was usually a cheerful sort of chap but today he looked glum.

'It's alright for you,' Puck grumbled. 'I've not been to see the parade. The officers have had all the civvies over in their wardroom for a reception and I've been washing up their party plates all afternoon. I've only just finished.'

Suddenly having stood out in the rain and getting a bit wet didn't seem quite so bad after all. Puck had not entirely escaped a soaking but he didn't get wet in quite the same manner as the rest of them. He had only got wet up to his elbows and his water was warm—if a little soapy.

A chap Ginger got talking to the day after the QBR had a different tale to tell about water and getting wet. He had never seen this boy before, in fact there was no reason why he should have. It transpired that he was several recruitments ahead of the current inmates of the Annexe and well established over in the main establishment.

This particular day, quite by chance he was on the sports field and leaning up against the Annexe perimeter fence when it so happened that Ginger was in the same place but on the Annexe side of the fence. Whether that fence was there to keep the nozzers in or the established hands of the main out was not

49

clear. No-one had ever mentioned it, until now Ginger had not even noticed that there was a fence.

They got talking and the lad said his name was Derek Squires. He spoke with a West Country accent and said he was in Anson Division. Ginger gave no indication that he hadn't heard of Anson and had no idea where it was. That side of the road was still a mystery to him and as far as he was concerned, it might as well have been on the other side of the world.

Derek seemed a pleasant enough sort of chap and a chat with a stranger made a nice change. They soon established that Derek was training to be a bunting-tosser—a flag signalman—and today his mess was playing cricket. He explained that he didn't like cricket very much and hadn't been picked to play. Those not actually playing had to come to the sports field to watch, he said.

Ginger noticed that Derek was completely at ease and enjoying his afternoon sports break; there was no tension and no nervous looking over his shoulder to see if anyone was coming.

So, from that observation he deduced that things must be far more relaxed over there, unlike the Annexe where you were watched almost continually from the moment you got out of bed until you got back in it again something like fifteen hours later.

He felt pretty secure as well on this particular afternoon because Bumble had told them to spend the afternoon in the mess sewing over the remainder of their names with the red silk. But then he had made the mistake of saying he would be back at tea time, which in effect, although he hadn't actually said so, told them that he wouldn't be around for about three hours.

The instructor boy was also busy. He had just been issued with his tropical kit and he was far too preoccupied with his own problems to worry about what anyone else was doing. Armed with that information Ginger decided that this was a golden opportunity to wander about and do nothing and that was how he came to be behind the mess blocks and near the perimeter fence.

They had gone through the almost standard routine of: 'How long have you been in? .... What mess are you in? .... What's it like over there?'

Pretty standard questions that, give or take a little, received something close to standard replies. The faces changed but, in general, the questions remained the same over the years.

After a while the subject got around to the QBR and how it had rained all the time. Ginger commented on how unusual it was to see so much rain. Everything had been soaked with puddles everywhere; every dip in the ground had been turned into a miniature lake.

Derek could now go into his 'old hand' routine, Ginger had given him the perfect opening. For some reason all Ganges boys loved to play the old hand. In extreme cases one boy might only be six weeks ahead of another, but that would be enough to give him a superior feeling and enough authority to try on his storm tossed veteran routine. Even the meekest of the timid would try it on; they were usually a bit more cautious about it, for fear of ridicule but they would try it on just the same, whenever the opportunity presented itself.

It was almost like some kind of illness. Like an alcoholic with drink, or a compulsive gambler with betting, they just had to try it on; everybody did it, it was part of Ganges life.

Derek didn't appear to be a 'bighead' or one of the real old hand brigade, but this was too good an opportunity to miss. A chance to swing-that-lamp to a green nozzer.

'You think that was a lot of water. You should have been here a few months back, we had water then all right,' he said.

Ginger was all ears. 'Why, what happened. What do you mean?'

'There had been some terrible flooding along the East Coast and we had to go out and help with the rebuilding of the sea walls, where the sea had broken through.'

This was incredible. They had actually got away from that place and away from instructors. He wanted to know more.

'But why you .... how did you know .... who told you ....' the questions came tumbling out without a pause for an answer.

'Our instructor, a chief yeoman got us out of bed as usual one morning and told us to put on overalls and that we were going to work instead of instructions. They said some other classes had already gone to assist, but they needed more help.'

Derek was matter of fact in his story telling. He was telling the truth but at the same time had that feeling of superiority that comes from relating your experiences to a complete nozzer.

Ginger was there; he was totally captivated. It was like a war film. There they were, sailors doing men's work, not boys being shouted at. They were saving the poor country people from being flooded out. He could imagine himself working hard and laughing with the locals, they would treat him like a man. They would call him to help an old lady into the rescue boat; they would stand and cheer when he saved a small baby from drowning

'Go on, go on. What did you have to do?' he asked impatiently.

'We had to fill sandbags with mud and rebuild the sea walls,' Derek explained, he had already said that once. Now he couldn't help embellishing.

'It was really hard work and it went on all week. At the end of each day we returned to Ganges absolutely knackered and after a shower and a meal we went to bed and slept like dead men until the morning.'

'One thing I remember particularly', continued Derek, 'no-one ever mentioned hygiene. When dinner arrived it was a cup of soup and sandwiches, or an oggie. We had to eat where we were and when we had finished the soup out of our tin mugs, we washed them out in the flood water.'

'Cor,' said Ginger, almost hero worshipping his new friend. 'I bet you got treated well when all that work was finished, like a bit of time off or a bit of extra leave, to make up for all the extra time you worked.'

'You would have thought so wouldn't you,' said Derek gloomily. 'But not a chance. We finished with the floods on Friday and then they told us that we were guard class the following week. That meant we had to turn to all weekend to learn the necessary drills required to enable us to do guard duty for the daily Divisions.'

Ginger had already learnt enough about daily Divisions to know what that must have entailed. After all that hard work and so tired, it wouldn't have hurt them—whoever they were—to have picked another class for guard and let Derek's class have a weekend with nothing to do. After all, they deserved it.

They had Divisions in the Annexe every morning. It was a waste of time really, but never the less, every morning there they were out in front of the Divisional Office, all fell in and facing that little mast.

The first few days had been easy enough. But as soon as everybody had mastered the basic principles of parade ground drill, 'Divisions' dominated the start of every day. In those early days it was simple enough. Bumble taught his charges how to stand to attention and at ease, he also showed them how to turn right and left. Then, armed with that knowledge, they were ready for a crack at their first Divisions proper. Those first half a dozen Divisions were just a matter of standing in straight lines in their respective messes and being inspected by the Divisional Officer.

But Divisions it was. It entailed very little in the way of effort or thought as he already knew the basic stuff. It involved nothing more demanding than just standing around for a while the instructors did their own thing—accompanied by a lot of shouting—then standing to attention, standing at ease, then to attention again then finally turning left and marching away.

Then, after about a week of that, with Bumble teaching them more every day, it was decreed that they were ready for their first march past. Shamble past would have been a more accurate description, where even at this stage some of them hadn't grasped the fundamentals of everyone starting off on the same foot.

Most of them didn't know what they were doing, they were still concentrating on trying to keep in step or get the opposite arm to swing back as the leg stepped forward with each pace.

Ginger had been through all that basic stuff with the army cadets so he found it all straight forward and even a little boring. He helped to keep his interest alive by marvelling at some of the antics of his fellow mess mates. How some of them managed to get themselves into the most incredible amount of trouble just by executing even the easiest of manoeuvres, was beyond him.

But instead of putting himself forward as a possible example to help his new pals, he chose the easy route of losing himself in the middle of the centre rank and keeping out of harms way—and hopefully out of Bumble's sight. That green coat was getting bigger all the time.

Even the thickest of the thick had to get it right eventually, or if not exactly right then passable. Then, one morning, after about four weeks, they were told that they had progressed enough to warrant the Royal Marine Band coming over to the Annexe to teach them to march in time to the beat of a drum and music.

Marching to music made a nice change and it put new life into the step, it even managed to pull Ginger back from the depths of monotony.

They all appeared to be revitalised as they positively stamped up and down the length of the parade ground with the beat of the music ringing in their ears .... 'Life on the Ocean Wave .... Te Tiddley—Tiddley Tum ....'

Chapter 6

Finally the big day arrived.

That long anticipated moment was here at last. They had completed their basic induction training and were about to move over to the main establishment.

This was the day they had been eagerly awaiting. Utopia was just across the road, of that they were certain. The last four weeks of their six week stay in the Annexe, talk had been of very little else. Their time had been made a little more bearable by the certain knowledge that one day soon they would be out of that place and across the road where they would be treated like men. They all knew it. Everyone had been convincing everyone at every opportunity until it became a way-of-life, matter-of-fact statement. Yes, they told each other, for sure they would all be much better off once they were over the road and permanent residents of the main.

No-one questioned how any of them knew what it was like over there; they just knew. Probably it was just chief Bumble's words they had latched on to. Bumble had said weeks ago that things would be much better for them 'over there' and somehow those few words had become gospel. All the inhabitants of Jellicoe Two had grasped Bumbles words, like a drowning man grasping straws and they were all totally convinced.

Bumble had probably just said that to keep everyone happy until they were out of his care. He probably didn't even remember saying it. It was quite possibly the first thing that came into his head to stop discontentment setting in, or maybe it was a line used by all Annexe instructors.

Whatever the reason it was almost a certainty that the boys couldn't remember who said it, or why. It was just a plain straight forward statement of fact that everybody knew: things would be much better when they got over to the main—and now the big day had arrived.

A few of the more 'knowledgeables' knew days in advance. How they knew was never brought into question. They'd already been around spreading the 'buzz', so really it was no great surprise when Bumble made the news official.

The buzz spreaders were from Beatty One mess; there was two of them.

Although they were still virtually green nozzers, Ginger had learned enough to know that buzz spreaders and trouble makers always worked in pairs. He knew this pair. It was Lowley and 'Shiny' Black.

They had come down on the train from Norwich with him. He remembered Lowley particularly because when the recruiter had asked if anyone knew the way to the station, Lowley had jumped up and volunteered to lead the squad of about ten of them down to catch their train.

Lowley was a bit of a scruff then. That day in the recruiting office he was wearing an old casual shirt and a pair of plimsoles. He stood out partly through his mode of dress and partly because he had a kind of ingratiating authority about him.

'Yes sir, I know the way sir. Yes sir, I'll be careful sir.'

'I'll look after them sir,' he had assured the recruiter, without showing a hint of embarrassment in front of the others. But, true to his word, he did know the way.

Lowley had probably used the same technique on the Beatty mess instructor. That man seemed a bit more approachable than Bumble and quite possibly Lowley had used his 'charm' to be given a preview of their future movements. Now he was using his newly found information to gain popularity with the boys of other messes.

Lowley and Black were complete opposites in every way. Lowley was fairly tall and well built. He had a pale pasty complexion and long straggly hair that hung down covering most of his face—or at least he did have long blond hair until the Annexe barbers got to work on it.

By contrast 'Shiny' Black was skinny and shorter. He had darker skin and short, dark curly hair. Their personalities were completely opposite too.

Lowley had a way of being noticed. He always seemed to be in the centre of things; he was almost without shame and couldn't understand a snub or the cold shoulder treatment. He would force his way into a group of people and then talk continuously in that particular manner of his.

Black, on the other hand, had no personality at all, or at least nothing discernable. He had no voice to speak of and, apparently, no opinions other than those imposed by Lowley. He would follow Lowley about like a little puppy dog agreeing without hesitation to whatever Lowley's thoughts on a current project might be.

'Yes, Lows mate, certainly Lows mate. I'll do that for you Lows mate,' he would snivel, rubbing his hands together in the manner of Uriah Heap, the Dickens character.

Occasionally when Lowley had the attention of a group, like when he imparted the news of their impending draft to the main, Black would worm in and out of the gathering whining his little gems. 'You'd better listen when Lowley's talking. Lowley knows what he's talking about.'

His bravery level rose considerably when Lowley was in close attendance.

Forewarned with Lowley's advance information, a few of the boys started preparing their kit ready for packing away, but Ginger was having none of that. Bumble would tell them what to do when the time was right and in any case they were never quite sure what they would be expected to wear, sometimes from one hour to the next, so it was no use packing too much anyway. He noticed that the majority of his messmates had made no positive move along those lines either and that made him feel confident that he had made the right decision. In fact he knew he was right.

As luck would have it they were not subjected to any unnecessary changes of kit, in fact Bumble even went as far as to make the concession of letting them sleep in their underwear on their last night in his care, so that even their pyjamas could be washed and rolled up ready for that final Annexe kit inspection.

That last kit inspection was passed with flying colours by everyone, not that there was any reason for it to be otherwise. They had all been issued with a brand new kit only about six weeks previously and with the eagle eyes of either Bumble or Chalkie White on them at all times, there had not been long enough for anything to get worn or dirty.

Bumble had spent considerable time demonstrating how kit should be rolled up around a bit of cardboard and tied with bits of string, known as clothes stops, at each end so that the newly sewn in names were showing exactly in the centre. Chalkie White had ensured that no item of kit in the entire Annexe would be left dirty.

Throughout their stay in the Annexe, Chalkie had been regarded with a mixture of emotions: suspicion, hatred and fear being the predominant ones. The precise percentage of each depended upon the individual and how easily they had adapted to Chalkies regime. Ginger had somehow managed to evade that strip of wood of his and, to some extent, he had been lucky in that he had never incurred Chalkies full wrath, although he had seen it vented on others— and that was close enough.

However, now the big day was here. The final kit inspection was over and their sessions with Chalkie were well behind them. As they mustered outside Jellicoe Two for the last time Chalkie was nowhere to be seen; pretty soon he would be forgotten and, with a bit of luck, never seen again.

Everything they owned fitted into their kitbag; even the small attaché case, gas mask and oilskin coat went inside. Bumble had ensured everything was packed in the correct order by calling out one item at a time. That particular item of kit had to be held up and then placed into the kitbag on his command. Boots and rolled up blue suits in the bottom, followed by the remainder of the kit in sequence until the little attaché case went on top, followed lastly by the tin hat box, with the gas mask and tin hat on the very top.

The kitbags then had to be carried outside and stacked up on the parade ground. By this time the boys had been told what their new mess would be over the road and kitbags were stacked in heaps corresponding to the new messes.

Not everyone from Jellicoe Two was going to the same place, some of the brighter ones would be forming an AC mess. Ginger was glad that he would remain with most of the people he had got to know during their time together. He didn't know what AC was in any case, in fact he was to learn that it simply meant Advanced Class; some of the ex-Grammar School types and the like that had a higher academic level.

That was all sorted out when they did a written test earlier on. Ginger would be going to Hawke 49 mess. He was assigned 61 class. 62 class would also be in 49 mess.

Big Humph, the boxer, Jasper and Puck were heading for the AC mess wherever that might be and would hardly ever be seen again. Ginger was relieved to notice that Mick Southern would be going to Hawke with him. Mick was a good bloke and although Bumble hadn't given them much time for forming friendships, he liked Mick, they seemed to hit it off right from the start. Dereham, a big burly chap who had come down from Norwich on the train that first day, would be going to Hawke.

It was a good feeling to know that he wouldn't be chucked in with a bunch of strangers, although only a matter of six weeks ago they were all strangers. Doug Raines and Ray Leeward were a couple more that were going to Hawke.

Ray was another that was OK; he didn't say a lot but neither did Ginger. That was probably the reason they had drifted together. Doug, by contrast, had an outgoing personality, he was Rays pal really and although they were all more or less of the same age, Doug, a Londoner, seemed years older. Londoners, for some reason, seemed to think that they were better than everyone else. It certainly was the case as far as Doug was concerned, he'd learned the art of wearing his hat at a rakish angle and despite being in the Navy all of six weeks he had taken on all the appearances of an old salt.

It was undoubtedly Doug's cavalier attitude that was his undoing. That, coupled with his 'old sea dog' appearance, got him singled out right away by their new instructors.

Kitbags were stacked in piles according to their new destination and for some reason the boys who would form those new messes were allowed to congregate around their respective piles. No-one actually told them to, they were just drawn in part to what represented their new home and partly to keep their eye on their kit.

It was unusual for the Navy to allow people just to wander about and stand in small groups. No-one said 'fall-in' and they took advantage of this lapse. Anyway they were old hands now; they'd completed their training and the Annexe instructors knew that. That was probably the reason they were allowed to act in this informal manner.

They were not aware of it at this stage but what they were waiting for was for the transport to take their kit over to their new messes in the Main.

Also what they didn't know was that their new instructors were on their way over to meet them for the first time.

With all the milling around and the excited conversations going on, they failed to see the two instructors for Hawke 49 mess approaching. If the boys had seen them it wouldn't have helped very much, they didn't know who they were anyway. That was soon to change. They were quickly informed and Doug in particular was to gain first hand knowledge.

Their new instructors were completely different. Different from each other and entirely different to the Annexe instructors. Where Bumble had demonstrated slowly and patiently how to do things, sometimes over and over again, the new men were having none of that; they were businesslike and abrupt, particularly Geoff Leverett.

Leverett was an acting petty officer and still wore the square rig, the same as the boys, except that he had crossed anchors on his sleeve. He didn't look very friendly and quickly he was to confirm that he wasn't very friendly. He was a tall, thin, ginger-haired man. His face was thin which made his bones stick out giving him a hard chiselled appearance. His eyes bulged out and he had the knack of staring, not so much at them but right through them. He had a way of speaking through clenched teeth.

As he drew level with his new charges, his voice rasped out.

'Who told you to speak?'

His voice was as formidable as his appearance. He wasn't addressing anyone in particular. It was his way of demanding silence. But poor old Doug just had to be the one to speak.

It wasn't that Doug was having a bout of defiance, he was talking and hadn't quite finished what he was saying. He hadn't heard Leveretts demand for their full attention.

Acting Petty Officer Leverett had instantly got everyone's attention except Doug. Doug was only talking quietly but Leverett leapt straight at him.

'You got something to say lad?'

Doug, caught unawares, mumbled something and suddenly found something very interesting with his feet.

'What's your name lad?'

Again Doug mumbled something but that was not enough to satisfy Leverett. His face turned bright red with anger. He looked ready to explode.

'Find your kitbag then, maybe we'll find your name on that.'

Doug quickly found his kitbag and pulled it out of the heap. He dragged it across to where their new instructor was standing. At Leverett's feet he turned the bag so that the bottom with the name showing could be seen.

'Not like that lad, up here where I can see it.'

Doug struggled to lift the heavy bag up to shoulder height as Leverett was indicating.

'That's better lad, now I can see it.'

He made Doug stand in front of him with the heavy bag on his shoulder while he read out the letters slowly and deliberately.

'R–A–I–N–E–S'

Each letter was accompanied by a long pause and a sneer.

'Raines, huh. It doesn't rain until I say so.'

That was his concession at a joke. Doug didn't get the joke, his face was red from exertion and he looked on the verge of dropping his load.

'Now, while you've got it on your shoulder take it for a trip round the parade ground—at the double and think about keeping silence next time.'

It was not that Doug had done anything wrong. Leverett had come over determined that he would stamp his authority on things from the very beginning and Doug had fallen easy prey. It could have quite easily been any of them. As Doug tramped around the parade ground in the heat, embarrassed to be in full view of the entire inhabitants of the Annexe, the boys of Hawke 49 mess were thanking their lucky stars it wasn't them.

Leverett had made his point. The boys had all got the message, Doug most of all.

Petty Officer Jury was the other instructor. Up until this point he had not said a word. Now he spoke for the first time.

'Right then. Hawke 49, fall in here.'

Cyril Jury spoke in much softer tones. After Leverett's tirade Cyril Jury was like a breath of fresh air. His face was more relaxed; he showed no emotion, either good or bad. He was matter of fact but not intimidating like Leverett.

Jury wore the fore and aft rig of an established Petty Officer. His badges denoted that he was a three badge PO GI. GIs—Gunnery Instructors—were known for their ability to shout and Jury soon proved that he was no exception.

What was exceptional, or at least unusual, was that when he shouted it was for a reason and not in anger. Petty Officer Jury had a lot going for him in the boys eyes but what stood out above everything else was his smartness and bearing.

Everyone in Ganges was obliged to conform to an unusually high standard of dress and cleanliness. They insisted everybody maintained a high standard, trainees, ships company and instructors. But Cyril Jury stood out among people where high standards were normal. He was immaculate in dress, bearing and, they were to learn, efficiency too.

Although he had only spoken a few words, there was something about him that they sensed immediately. He spoke with authority and he commanded respect. The boys of Hawke 49 respected him from that very first meeting.

They respected him and what's more—they liked him.

Petty Officer Jury called his new charges to attention and they were on their way.

Leaving their kitbags behind they wheeled left round the postie's shack and headed out of the gate, just as they had on the previous occasions when they had travelled to the main.

This time it was different. This time they wouldn't be coming back

By the time they had marched off Doug had off loaded his kitbag and had tagged on the back of the squad, on Leverett's orders.

PO Jury had marched them off and now, just outside the gate, Leverett was back in control. It was his voice calling out the step as they headed for the Main Gate.

He had a loud voice. Ever since they had first heard him speak he had shouted at full volume. How he managed to shout so loudly through clenched teeth was a mystery. He had large teeth that remained together even when he was shouting; only his lips moved. Not so much moved but curled back in a snarl.

Ginger couldn't see him as they marched along, but he could picture him: slightly leaning forward, bright red in the face with his hat crammed right down almost to his ears and the veins on his neck inflated almost to bursting point, as he screeched out the step.

'Leefe .... Arr .... Leefe .... Arr'

He couldn't sound the 'T' at the end of his words without opening his teeth.

They followed the same route as they did when they came over to climb the mast and for the swimming test, but this time there was absolute silence from the ranks. The only sound was Leverett's voice. They had not heard such a carry on before, he had been shouting continuously.

60

Bumble used to give matter of fact orders and then, if they'd got it wrong, he would call them to a halt and explain as many times as it took, until they all had it right. If they thought Bumble was hard, Leverett was something else.

They'd had a never ending stream of venom all the way across.

'Get your arm up shoulder height, not swinging about like bloody windmills regulation paces lad, don't mince along like your old granny. ..'

These gems were punctuated at intervals by his 'Leefe .... Arr .... Leefe .... Arr' until they were in the Main Gate.

They wheeled left at the corner of the guardhouse but instead of turning right at the edge of the parade ground, they carried straight on ahead. As they reached the parade ground, there came a new order.

'Double March.'

They broke into the double and headed diagonally across, toward the swimming bath. When they came over for the swimming test they had gone round so as not to go on the parade ground. But this time, under Leveretts guidance, they were going straight across the centre.

As they made their way toward the swimming bath, some two story old tin shacks would be the first thing they reached. Those old shacks turned out to be their new home—Hawke Division.

Hawke consisted of five messes; two double stories with a single story mess in between. In front and covering the full width was an open fronted walkway similar to that in front of the Annexe messes.

As they came parallel to that walkway, Leverett screeched out one word: 'Halt.'

Somehow he had managed to pronounce the 'T' this time. He was still quite a way off because had hadn't doubled with the boys. They stood still not daring to move or look round to see where he was. Then as he drew level, his next words came as a big surprise.

'Right then lads, fall out and wait for your kit under the walkway.'

For a few seconds no-one moved. Maybe it was a trick; maybe he hadn't said that; maybe someone was playing about, but sure enough it was Leverett. His voice still rasped, his teeth still looked as formidable as ever, but he had said fall out and so they did.

A couple of the boys made slight movements just to test the situation then, as Leverett made no attempt to stop them, the remainder moved as one and very quickly they were all on the concrete floor of the walkway.

PO Jury had long since disappeared. They hadn't seen him since they left the Annexe and now Leverett looked like he had something better to do.

'OK then, wait here until your kit arrives and then take it up to 49 mess—

that's the one on the top end over there,' he said, pointing to the top left hand block. 'I'll be back to sort things out in a few minutes.' With that he turned abruptly on his heels and walked towards what they were to learn was the POs' block, without another word and without once looking back.

Left to their own devices was a new experience, this was the first time they had been completely alone. The whole place seemed to be deserted there wasn't a soul anywhere. They were outside 47 mess, the single story one. There was no-one in there either.

Maybe the main was the place to be; maybe now they had moved over here permanently they were allowed to do what they liked. If this was the Annexe there would have been Bumble hovering over them. Apparently they were men now and didn't need continual supervision.

Leverett said that they should take their kit up to 49 mess when it arrived so there should be no reason why they couldn't go up now and take a look at their new living quarters. There was nothing else to do so Ginger decided to investigate.

Inside the front door there was a small storeroom to the left and just beyond was the stairs that led up to 49 mess. The stairs were in three sections leading behind and eventually above the storeroom.

He ascended the stairs in a state of anticipation. As he turned left at the top there was a small room with a toilet and sink directly to his right and that was followed by a large washroom with a big black marble slab, stretching the full length of the far wall. This took up all the right hand side leading down to the messdeck.

Opposite the washroom, on the left hand side of the passage, was an airing room, just a big empty room with hot pipes running all around it. The airing room and the stairs took up all that side of the passage.

He was not very impressed by what he saw. It was almost identical to Jellicoe Two, back in the Annexe. Quite what he expected it to be like he didn't know, somehow he felt sure it would be different; better hopefully, but certainly different. He had climbed those stairs with boyish enthusiasm in anticipation of something, although he didn't know what.

It was a bit like that Christmas feeling. The anticipation builds up and although you don't really know why, you expect something wonderful; although you don't need anything, you still look forward to receiving presents. This was that kind of feeling. He didn't know what he expected he just knew it would be something, a sense of occasion at the very least.

Having taken all of thirty seconds to climb those stairs, glance in the washroom, the airing room and the messdeck, he now felt cheated.

It was as if Father Christmas didn't come after all. He didn't want anything; he didn't know what he expected to feel. Surely there should have been a warm glow, or some sort of good feeling at least. After all this was to be his home for the next twelve months.

There was nothing. It was just an empty barrack block. His bubble burst, his good feelings evaporated; he felt deflated, absolutely dejected. He was the only one interested enough to go up for a sneak preview and it was nothing.

He quickly descended the stairs and joined the others waiting outside without saying a word.

Chapter 7

By the time the kit had arrived, been unloaded from the lorry and Leverett had returned from wherever it was that he was in such a hurry to get to, it was getting close to midday. What, up until then, had been a relaxed atmosphere now took on an air of urgency.

'Right then, stop cackling your fat and pay attention.'

This was the Leverett of old back again. This was the Leverett of their first meeting. Gone was the Leverett of twenty minutes ago, who had told them to wait under the walkway for their kit.

Ginger had began to form a different opinion of him from that. He thought that maybe all that shouting was for the benefit of the Annexe instructors. But now he quickly changed his mind back again.

Leverett hadn't changed. He hadn't mellowed in the least.

It was as if his power source had run down and he'd gone away for another injection of venom. He was now back to full strength, the way they remembered him when he had torn into poor old Doug for no reason. As one man, Hawke 49 silently vowed to always regard him the way he was right now. He was egotistical, spiteful and downright nasty. Provided they always remembered that and dealt with him accordingly, then maybe, just maybe, they might survive their year intact under his control.

Petty Officer Jury they liked. Although they had only met him for a brief few moments, they liked him. Unlike Leverett, they hadn't known him any longer but they had already convinced themselves that they disliked him.

First impressions are usually correct and in Leverett's case they certainly were

In the space of time it took them to march from the Annexe to their new home, they could hardly have formed a hatred of the man, but they certainly disliked him. They had more or less instantly disliked him but more to the point, they all feared him.

They were far too intimidated to show airy sign of opposition though. They could hardly ignore him or give him the cold shoulder; he was far too awesome to try on anything so obvious. They had a year stretching out ahead of them and Leverett would always be there. When he said 'jump' they would jump. They didn't have to like it but they would do it. They didn't have to like him but they would have to tolerate him.

Leverett had got everyone's attention. After his earlier performance over in the Annexe, he only had to clear his throat now and everyone jumped three feet.

'Kitbags up to the mess. Find yourselves a bed and put the kitbag on it, then back down here as quickly as you can. Come on. Move.'

That was quite a mouthful for him. So far he had only rasped out short sharp sentences. Either way his orders were clear and away they went.

Ginger had already spotted his kitbag and as soon as Leverett gave the word, he was away. He knew the way up the stairs and he knew which was his kitbag, so he was one of the first to enter their new mess at the top of the stairs.

Something, instinct probably, drew him to the left and he dumped his load down on the first vacant bed that came to hand.

It just happened to be the fourth bed along on the left, a similar position to that he had occupied in Jellicoe Two. He noticed some of the others running the full length of the mess to grab the beds up at the far end, probably looking for the same position they had in the Annexe as well.

Dump their kitbags and get back downstairs and outside, was what Leverett had ordered and no-one wanted telling twice. They knew he was waiting for them down below. Ginger was the first back as he'd had a head start on most of the others. In fact on his way down he passed some of the boys still going up, but straight away he could tell Leverett was getting impatient.

They couldn't possibly have been any quicker. It was straight up to the mess, dump the bag and back down again at the double. There was no time to stop and look around or get a bed next to your mate unless you were lucky enough to have come in at the same time and find a couple of adjacent spare beds.

But never the less, apparently that was not quick enough for Leverett. He was stamping up and down and looking very agitated.

'Fall in three deep,' He yelled over the din of hobnailed boots crashing down the wooden stairs. 'Come on, fall in and STAND STILL.'

A matter of only seconds later he had three smart ranks of boys, standing properly at ease, facing their new mess and as quickly as the noise had started, it had stopped and there was complete silence.

'Right then, it's dinner time. I'll show you where Hawke section is. I'll show you once so pay attention. Right then. Class Sharrr. Right turn. Double march.'

They wheeled slightly to get out from under the walkway—Leverett had called it the colonnade—and headed diagonally across the parade ground, retracing their route from the Annexe.

At the far end of the parade ground, he rasped in that particular way of his: 'Quick March'. They slowed to the quick march and then, instead of going round the corner to the guard house and main gate they turned in behind it and on to a paved area that led alongside the new dining hall. They followed the paving right down to the far end, leaving the playing fields to their right as they went. At the bottom Leverett called them to a halt.

They were the only ones marching down there, everyone else was just walking along in small groups talking and laughing with each other. Some of the laughter was probably directed at them. Everyone knew they just had to be nozzers straight over from the Annexe. If there was any doubt before, there wasn't any now. Leverett had seen to that by making them march round.

He stood glaring at them for a few seconds and then turned and walked toward the entrance door.

'Right then. Fall out and follow me.'

The boys obediently followed him like little sheep, not knowing what they were about to encounter.

In through the double doors they went and across the small entrance lobby. Inside a second set of double doors they were faced with rows and rows of tables stretching away into the distance, the full length of the building. As luck would have it, Hawke Division tables were the first ones inside the door.

'Sit down at those empty tables,' said Leverett, 'eat yer grub and then get back and stow your kit away.'

With that he turned on his heels and was gone.

The place had been filling up while Leverett had been sorting them out and the new boys in a new place seated themselves, as instructed, eight to a table and waited to be served with their first meal in 'the main'. Pretty soon the place was alive with boys running about with wire baskets full of plates of dinner. The baskets were the same as those use in the Annexe and just for a fleeting second Ginger had visions of that first meal over there, when he had to be 'duty cook'. This time things were different and they didn't have to get the food themselves. Streams of boys appeared from somewhere carrying the dinners and each 'carrier' served a table.

The CMG, or Central Mess Galley, was an impressive building. It was the dining hall for all the boys. They were served on two floors; each division had their own section. It had been open for about a year and was still as good as brand new.

It was officially opened by the C-in-C Nore, Admiral Sir Cecil Harcourt, on June 12 the previous year, almost a year to the day. The publicity said it was the 'largest and most modern in use in the Royal Navy—and would remain a showpiece for many years to come.'

It was certainly impressive right enough. Everything was spotlessly clean with Formica topped tables, unlike the Annexe tables which were plain wood and had to be scrubbed.

They reckoned that an everyday menu would need, among other things, 19 cwts of potatoes; 400 pounds of beef; 500 pounds of fish; 18,000 slices of bread; 224 pounds of sugar and 36 pounds of tea.

But despite that amount of food to be prepared every day, the boast was that each galley could turn out a three-course meal, soup, main course and sweet for 2,000 people that could be served and eaten within twenty minutes.

In addition to the good side there was a down side. It was said that during their first month of operation, 1,000 cups and 1,000 plates were broken. A notice to that effect was on display. It also stated that in future breakages would have to be paid for. But by the time the new nozzers arrived they had at least solved the problem of breaking cups. They didn't supply any. Every boy had to use his own tin mug.

They were proud of their new 'showpiece' and were ready to trot out facts at every opportunity.

The CMG was built, they said, on a site formerly occupied by two officers tennis courts, behind the guardhouse. It was two stories high with a large basement. The two stories contained the two dining halls, with an all-electric galley on each floor.

The basement was split into three sections. One was the rum store, although the boys never got any of that. Another was for the calorifiers and steam heated storage tanks; the third section was a rainwater storage tank, capable of holding 125,000 gallons of water collected from the roof and the surrounding paved areas. They reckoned that 11,000 gallons of water was used every day. What was not used for drinking went for food preparation and washing-up.

The electric loading of the CMG was estimated to be more than the rest of the establishment put together, therefore, to cope, a separate sub station had to be built.

Other useless facts that were to turn up from time to time included the 245 tons of steel work used in the construction of the building; 50,000 cubic feet of concrete; 5,000 square yards of tiling for floors and walls and, perhaps the only fact that was of the remotest interest to the boys, the 900 square yards of glass for the windows. The reason why that got everyone's attention was each one cost six shillings to replace—as a few of the more expert cricketers had already found to their cost.

They certainly thought a lot of their new 'showpiece' and although it had been open and in constant use for more than a year, those facts were still trotted out at the drop of a hat.

None of the new boys were particularly interested, their main concern was getting their dinner down their throats. Although the CMG was similar to the Annexe dining hall, albeit the Annexe one was very much smaller, the atmosphere was a lot more relaxed than it was back there. All Annexe meals were eaten under the gaze of some instructor or other and in the very early days, more than one. But today there was not an instructor to be seen and the new inhabitants of 49 mess enjoyed their first unsupervised meal together.

Maybe this was another of the Navy ways.

They had finished their training and now they had come over to the main and joined the Navy proper.

In the Annexe they had been shown what to do at every step of the way, but now that their training was over maybe the Navy expected them to remember and act without supervision. They were in the main now and it was much better over here, they all knew that. Over here they would be treated like men.

The lack of supervision did nothing for their table manners however and the meal was grabbed and scoffed in record time, with the sweet suffering the same fate. There was no reason to eat that quickly; it just seemed the natural thing to do. There was absolutely no hurry really, after all they had more than an hour for the dinner break at midday but ever since their involvement with the Navy on day one, six weeks ago, all meals had been demolished at breakneck speed.

Maybe there was some form of subconscious justification for the high speed gastronomic annihilation of everything in front them though because, they had learned that eating at a more leisurely pace would give the bully boys a chance to finish their meal first and then their attention would be diverted to someone else's plate.

'Don't you want that spud then?' would be accompanied simultaneously by a stab with a fork or a grab by a grubby hand.

It had not happened to Ginger up until now but he, like the vast majority of them, was leaving nothing to chance. Trying to fend off an intruder was a waste of time, because repelling someone to the right would allow a foreign fork from the left to sneak in.

Sometimes a more brazen bully type would be more open about it and his greedy voice would command: 'Hoy, gis that banger here.'

Occasionally, having eaten their own meal, they would walk past a table on their way to the door and just reach over and help themselves off some poor unfortunates plate. Any attempt at defiance or retaliation would serve no purpose because 'bully-boy' would be waiting outside and they always had at least two hangers-on who would help their 'mate' deal with anyone misguided enough to expect to eat all their own meal.

Ginger wasn't particularly a fighter, he'd confirmed that during the boxing tournament, but at the same time he wasn't prepared to let anyone else help him to eat his meagre plateful. They certainly were never over fed; there was just enough at each meal to carry them along to the next one. They certainly couldn't afford to miss a meal—or let someone else eat it for you.

He would have been prepared to fight if necessary, although it would have been a waste of time. Fighting wouldn't have got the pilfered grub back and while the scuffle was under way someone would steal the remainder, or it would get knocked over in the struggle. Either way it would mean a lost meal.

No, he had come up with a much better way. Eat everything placed in front of you and eat it as quickly as possible. That plan he had formulated within his first couple of days and, coupled with his natural talent for keeping a low profile, it had served him well. To date he had not had to fight anyone off and had not missed a meal.

He had seen others getting the treatment and losing some of their food. He would have liked to help them, but in all probability they would have been too intimidated to help themselves even with his help.

In any case it would have meant leaving his own plate unattended and that was something he would never do and in the second place, he wasn't a fighter. Most of the people that were picked on wouldn't help themselves anyway so if he went to their defence, he would have been on his own. So his plan had become to leave things alone and mind his own plate. He didn't like the situation but he resigned himself to minding his own business.

The obsession to eat at full speed had probably evolved over a period of time and somehow it carried over from one new entry intake to the next. Without realising why fully, all boys ate at full speed just to ensure they had something to eat.

Today, however, their first meal in the main was a comparatively relaxed affair. Maybe the bullies and the grabbers were taking things a bit easy until they had the situation worked out. There didn't appear to be any POs or chiefs about but the dining hall was a big place and until they were sure they were in the clear, it seemed they were not ready to take any chances.

Some of the bully-boys had lost their hangers-on to different divisions so they were on their own anyway and that may have curtailed their activities.

Most of the people here were senior and some of them badge boys; they might not be so easily terrorised.

Their first meal together in the CMG was a new experience. They were men now and over here, particularly in the dining hall, things were far more civilised. They were left on their own and expected to act responsibly.

Their first meal in their new surroundings was a far more relaxed affair but, partly through habit and partly to be on the safe side, they continued with their familiar routine and ate everything placed in front of them almost before the plate had touched the table.

This might be the main and things might be different over here but until they were sure, they were taking no chances

The people that were doing the fetching and carrying for them were called servers. They established that from their table server. He told them that each class had a turn at being server class for a week, sometime during their year and their turn would come in due course. He didn't appear to be in such a hurry to eat his dinner and, having learned from him that they were free to go when they had finished, they left him on his own to finish his dinner and clear the table.

Back outside they retraced their steps up alongside the dining hall and toward the southern end of Nelson Hall, where Leverett had brought them in.

'You the new Hawke mess?'

They stopped and looked round to see who had said that. There was a squad of about ten of them, just ambling along quite happy in the knowledge that Leverett had gone and they were on their own.

It was something of a rare occurrence to be left alone. This was only the second time in their six weeks that it had happened and both of these rare occasions had come within the last hour. This was new territory for them; they were just beginning to enjoy their new found freedom—and now this.

The idle chatter died away as they turned to face the direction of the enquirer. He was a fairly tall, well-built chap, with a strong booming voice. It was difficult to tell how old he was. He wore the same rig as them number eights, boots and gaiters. But who was he. They had only known Annexe instructors and instructor boys and they wore blue suits all the time. No-one only the boys had worn working dress over there.

Ginger's natural self-preservation came to the fore. Who is he? Is he an Instructor Boy? Maybe an instructor? What does he want? What have we done?

They stood waiting, looking a bit sheepish. Should they stand to attention, should they speak, should they address him as 'sir', maybe it would be safer to let him speak first. Leverett had got them worked up into a right old state.

'1 saw you in the CMG, in Hawke section and as I hadn't seen you before. I guessed that you must be the new boys for 49 mess. I'm in 48 mess, underneath you.'

He bad a big round cheerful face and a big grin; he was just trying to be friendly. He was a boy the same as them.

Leverett had certainly got them keyed up. They really were on their nerve edges. Fancy having a mental breakdown because a stranger had spoken to them.

Ginger was the first to recover his composure.

'You flaming idiot, you nearly gave us all heart attacks,' he gasped breathlessly but with signs of relief showing all over his face.

'I'm sorry,' said the boy, the big grin still on his face. He knew Ginger hadn't meant his outburst to sound nasty and he accepted it the way it was intended.

'I don't know what's wrong with you lot, this is dinner time. You can do what you like until the afternoon bugle tells you it's time to fall in. I just thought that I would warn you that you're not allowed on the parade ground without an instructor with you and you lot seem to be heading that way. This is the best way to go. Follow me.'

Instead of going through the gap behind the guardhouse, he turned left and led them up behind Nelson Hall along the edge of the playing fields and eventually turning right at the north end, round the cricket pavilion, which led along the front of the POs' block, to Hawke.

The remainder of 49 mess had seen the detour made by the crowd Ginger was with and, as they left the dining hall, they followed on the same route.

Outside Hawke, the boy spoke again.

'That's the way to go. Just remember it because if you don't you'll be doubling round the parade ground if you get caught. Use this route all the time and you'll be OK.'

'But some of them were going out the bottom end,' interrupted Bolshi Beano. Back in the Annexe Bolshi had got his name through his contrary nature. Whatever he was told to do Bolshi would always want to do it a different way.

He never wanted to use the iron until someone else was using it; he never wanted to have a wash until all the bowls were being used and now they were being advised to steer clear of the parade ground, Bolshi wanted to go that way.

His name was Beaney really, but he insisted: 'Everybody calls me Beano, don't they'. The 'Bolshi' bit, the boys had tagged onto him from the very start.

'Those boys that are going that way live down that way. They will cut across the bottom edge of the parade ground and under the mast, then they will lose themselves down in the covered ways, where their messes are,' replied the boy from 48 mess defensively. 'I'm just trying to be helpful and help you stay clear of trouble until you learn the routine for yourselves. You can please yourself what you do.'

With that he walked into his mess and disappeared. Ginger never saw him again, or at least if he did, he didn't recognise him. By the same token the boy never made himself known to them again. He had helped them and disappeared. They didn't even know his name.

Anyway they had a lot to occupy their minds and that little episode, helpful and informative as it undoubtedly had been, was not a major milestone in their lives and up in 49 mess there was kit to be unpacked and stowed away in their lockers and sports rig to be changed into before Leverett came back.

'Best change into sports gear first,' suggested someone loud enough for them all to hear. 'That way at least we'll be in the correct rig of the day when it's time to fall in again.' That sounded like a good idea and the appropriate clothing was dug out.

PO Jury was the first back after dinner. As the bugle sounded over the Tannoy, calling for the afternoon muster, he appeared as if by magic.

'You heard it. Whotca waiting for. Fall in down below in the colonnade. Come on then. Chop, chop.'

By the time he had finished speaking they had all got the message and the majority of them were already on their way down the stairs, they didn't want telling twice. That was a legacy of their time spent with chief Bumble.

Down below all Hawke messes were busy falling in under the colonnade; each mess had their own spot and each mess was faced by their instructors.

An officer appeared from around the corner at the far end of the colonnade and things suddenly became very quiet. After a moments pause the silence was broken by the instructors calling their messes to attention and standing them at ease again after they had reported to the officer.

Having been given their orders by the officer each instructor doubled their mess away to their various sporting activities until only 49 mess was left.

By this time Leverett had arrived. He didn't say anything but the black cloud of doom and despondency that he always transmitted, descended over the boys.

'Right then. Now that we're alone I'll tell you we won't be going anywhere this afternoon. The DO will be coming round to talk to you in a minute, so we shall stay here until then.' PO Jury had things under control. He was matter-of-fact in his explanations but at the same time quite easy to understand. He had a way of explaining without intimidating.

Another officer appeared from the same direction that the first one had come. This one was a tall, young looking chap. He had two rings on his sleeves with pilot's wings above the top ring. PO Jury called the boys to attention and smartly marched over to the new man.

He stopped in front of the officer and saluted him. Bumble had taught them how to salute and they had gone over it time and time again until he was satisfied that they had got it right, so they knew how to salute correctly. They noted that PO Jury's salute was absolutely perfect, unlike that of the officer, who seemed fairly embarrassed to be centre of attention with all eyes on him.

They exchanged a few words, then Jury saluted again, turned about and marched back to where he had left the boys. He was an incredibly smart man. He stood correctly, he marched correctly, he saluted correctly. Everything about him was correct. Cyril Jury was the ideal Navy advertisement. He was perfection.

'49 mess, classes 61 and 62, this is your Divisional Officer, Lieutenant Cassidy,' Jury told them in his matter-of-fact way.

It was a fact and he relayed it as such. There was no need to elaborate. Even his manner of speech had been trained the naval way. Short clipped sentences; economy of words; straight to the point; no emotion; typical Navy.

'Er, yes. Thank you Petty Officer. Er, stand at ease please.'

The boys obediently stood at ease and instantly formed the opinion that this stumbling, bashful twit would be a pushover. He was a pilot so what would he know about boys training. They'd finished their training back in the Annexe. They probably knew more than he did. What could he teach them that they didn't already know.

'Er, my name is Cassidy as, er, the Petty Officer just said. I'm your divisional officer. It's my pleasure to welcome you as new members of the Division. Er, we're all new boys here together as, as, as it were and I erm, expect that we shall all learn together. Hawke Division is a very good Division and I expect us all to maintain the high standard set by our predecessors and, to that end, I will not tolerate bleached or light collars. I want you all to go away and pick out your darkest collar and keep it just for Sunday Divisions. That's all. May we all enjoy our stay here in Hawke. Er, thank you Petty Officer.'

After he had got over his early 'erms and ers' his speech got faster and faster and as soon as he had finished, he quickly walked away back from where he had come, looking relieved that his ordeal was over. PO Jury called the boys to attention and, without moving from where he was, saluted Cassidy's fast disappearing back.

'Right then, now we shall .... ,' began Jury before he was cut short.

'Just a moment, Petty Officer.'

That was the officer that had first appeared. All the time Cassidy had been waffling on, he had been standing to one side scowling deeply.

Where Cassidy was tall and fair haired with a pale complexion, this one was much shorter, dark haired and of a foreign looking appearance. He had one thin ring on his arm. He'd had a scowl on his face ever since he had first arrived and it was still there as though it was a permanent feature. When he spoke it was with a strong nasal almost German sounding voice and he made it clear that he didn't like boys. The feeling was mutual.

'What are you doing?' he demanded.

'Just about to dismiss the mess and have them work on stowing their kit away properly, 'till teatime, sir,' replied Jury looking a bit flushed at having his actions questioned.

'I have something to say to them first.'

'Yes, certainly sir. I'll wait,' replied Jury.

At that the thin ringer looked agitated and if it were at all possible, his scowl deepened.

Jury seemed reluctant to leave and faltered as if about to say something else but after another moment's hesitation, both he and Leverett saluted, turned about and walked off toward the POs' block.

The thin ringer stood watching them walk away, as if he was afraid they might change their mind and come back, but as soon as he was sure they had gone, he turned his attention to the boys.

'So you're the new boys from the Annexe,' he began.

He really did talk down through his nose and that gave him the most appalling accent.

He was horrible and shifty and he sounded a lot like the German spies in those old war films. The only difference between them and him was—they were acting and he meant it.

Now that he was on his own with the boys his voice grew much louder.

'So you know it all do you?' He was talking more for his own benefit than for theirs. 'You might think you do. We shall see.'

After that he had them marching up and down in the colonnade for more than an hour. There was no reason for it at all apart from the fact that he felt like being nasty. He was just a downright horrible man. They had done very little except march up and down for the past six weeks, so they knew what they were doing. All the same, up and down they went with that awful 'Kraut Voice' finding fault with every little thing.

They had heard of Attila the Hun, now they were acquainted with one of his disciples. His name was Batchelor. Batchelor the Bastard.

Chapter 8

'Wednesday night is pictures night over here in the main,' PO Jury told them. 'So don't get wandering off because I shall be back straight after supper to take you round to watch your 'Micky Ducks' and I don't want to have to wait for anyone.'

Looking back over the days events so far, Ginger reflected that they had actually done nothing at all really although until now, when he stopped to think about it, he hadn't realised it any more than he guessed any of the others had.

The Navy had this effect on their lives.

A lot of the time they had them running around in circles achieving nothing and unless someone actually stopped to think about it, then put his thoughts into words, they didn't even realise that was what they were doing.

Maybe this was a carefully worked out plan devised by the Navy.

Earlier all they had done was packed their kitbags and waited around on the Annexe parade ground. Then they had marched over to their new home in Hawke Division and, if it hadn't been for Batchelor doing his private little number on them in the colonnade, they would have been in 49 mess all afternoon just packing their kit into their lockers and generally keeping out of everyone's way.

Maybe this was a carefully worked out plan; a system devised so that nozzers on their first day out of the Annexe, would have a comparatively easy time to help their transition from what after all amounted to a nursery, into main stream Ganges. None of them would accept the Annexe was a nursery but the more he thought about it the more he was sure that he had figured it out.

He didn't know for certain but all the signs indicated that the nozzers always came over on a Wednesday, just before dinner. That thinking fitted in with what had happened so far. The routine appeared to be that the new boys would pack their kit in the morning then march over to their new messes in time for dinner in the CMG. That would give them all afternoon to themselves, to stow their kit away and get accustomed to their new home while everyone else was out of the way playing sports. Then in the evening they would have a picture show in Number One Gymnasium. That was what had happened to Ginger and the latest batch and it had worked well.

If indeed that was the standard procedure with each new recruitment as they finished Annexe training, then maybe the Navy wasn't so heartless after all. They had given them what amounted to a day off but at the same time, continuing their policy of keeping everyone off balance and running around like headless chickens at all times, no-one had told the boys. They'd had a day off in essence but not one of them had realised the fact.

Apart from the episode with Batchelor, they'd had a pretty easy day of it and in any case it was much better than chasing around in the heat or lining up for more of those jabs the sick bay seemed fond of dishing out.

Now they were going to round off their easy day with a trip to the gym to enjoy a film show and let tomorrow take care of itself.

Tomorrow was another day.

Suddenly an almighty crash shattered the quietness. The tranquillity of the early morning in the tropical harbour was blasted away and lost forever as the gangway tore loose from the ships side and collapsed in a cacophony of splintering wood and screeching metal.

Those two blokes in their tropical whites had taken the motorboat away from where they had been waiting alongside the pontoon by the carrier's gangway, but they had forgotten to let go their stern line. As the cox'n went hard over and gave it full revs, the line pulled taut and snatched the gangway away from the ships side, sending it crashing down onto the pontoon below.

Ginger jumped up with a start.

He'd been daydreaming a bit and hadn't noticed that stern line still attaching the back of the motorboat to the gangway. But that crashing snapped him wide-awake, it was loud enough to awaken the dead. Everyone on board must have heard it and he knew he should do something quickly before the captain came to investigate.

'You flaming idiot,' he shouted at the top of his voice. It was more a shout of startled reaction than anger, but nevertheless he left them in no doubt of his feelings. But then, on second thoughts, maybe he was being a bit harsh. They had enough trouble without him adding to it. He self-consciously looked round to see who, if anyone—apart from the boats crew—had heard his outburst.

He was wide-awake now.

Perhaps he had been caught napping but he was certainly wide-awake now all right.

As he turned to survey the scene of the devastation, the full truth—or horror—of the situation swept over him. The gangway had gone; the pontoon had gone; the motorboat had gone and there was no crew to be seen ....

It had all been a dream.

There was no gangway; there was no motorboat; there was no pontoon. That crashing was Leverett's idea of a joke. He'd sent an empty dustbin crashing and careering down the mess, clanging and banging as it bounced off the foot of beds as it sailed along.

Ginger was sitting bolt upright in bed, eyes big and round as saucers, his mouth was wide open. Those three little words of his were still ringing in his ears. Everyone in the mess was looking at him. But worse still, Leverett was standing alongside his bed, looming tall and menacing.

'Whatcha gotta say for yerself boy. Who's a flaming idiot then?'

A nervous titter rippled round the mess. Leverett loved an audience; he pulled himself up to his full height and turned round slowly with a false smile on his face, willing the boys to join in his fun of browbeating some poor unfortunate who had no defence against him. Leverett loved his little jokes. They were jokes all the time they were going his way but as soon as they fell flat, or someone dared to answer back, he would turn nasty and official in an instant.

No-one was prepared to applaud his little pantomime and he was met with blank stares. Already the boys of 49 mess knew enough about him not to join in or trust him.

Leverett's little joke had gained no support. He was losing face but more to the point, he was turning nasty. There was nothing funny any longer and turning his attention back to Ginger, he pushed his face right up close. His big teeth were snarling, his breath was hot and damp. Ginger was getting sprayed as he emphasised every word in that rasping manner of his.

'Well, come on then. Let's have you out of that stinking pit, before I toss you out.'

Even as he spoke, Ginger went sailing through the air to land in an untidy heap among blankets, mattress and pillow. Without waiting even an extra second, Leverett had upended his bed and dumped him on the deck.

Calling Leverett a flaming idiot wasn't a good idea, even though it wasn't him Ginger was addressing at the time. Leverett wasn't the type to forget things like that, but apparently revenge could wait. He'd lost the first round and now he had other things on his mind

'Well come on then lad, don't just sit there like a nun at a ....'

The rest was lost as something crossed his mind for a second, but apparently that could wait whatever it was.

'Come on then, come on,' he rasped, giving Ginger his attention once more. 'Let's get these blankets champhered up then. You've got a lot of catching up to do.'

Leverett was already dressed. He had washed and shaved and his boots were polished, ready for the day ahead.

'Right then. First two washed and dressed—over to the CMG with the mess fanny for kye and biscuits. Well, what yer all standing there for.'

Then, turning back yet again, he snarled quietly and almost privately—'I've told you once. Get that bedding squared away right now, unless you'd like to lay your kit our before breakfast.' As he strode along the mess with his hobnailed boots sounding very loud on the wooden flooring, his voice rang out once again. He had bumped into the frontrunners returning from the bathroom.

'Right then, you two. You're back from the bathroom first. Get over to the CMG. By the time I return I expect to see that fanny scrubbed out and all mugs washed up and stowed away.'

With that he marched along the passage, down the stairs and out the door.

The whole episode, from throwing the dustbin until he left the mess couldn't have exceeded two or three minutes but, as always whenever Leverett was around, it seemed a whole lot longer.

At the same moment as he descended the stairs, the Tannoy buzzed into life with the bugler playing 'Charlie', their wake-up call. Their first 'Charlie' in the main.

The time was 0600.

Tomorrow certainly was another day and now it was here. It heralded the start of the rest of their lives in the Navy. It also introduced them to a sentence of twelve months and no prospect of time off for good behaviour.

It was less than twenty four hours since they had come over from the Annexe and about half of that time had been taken up by sleeping, so they hadn't had much of a chance to perform any kind of behaviour immaterial of whether it was good or bad. Nevertheless the general opinion of the place, or what they had seen of it so far, painted a far from rosy picture.

By Ganges standards they'd had an easy time of it up until now, comparatively speaking, despite the efforts of Leverett and Batchelor to make them feel otherwise. But, as with their first couple of days in the Annexe, they had nothing to compare. So they were not to know if it was easy or not.

It was too early to feel sorrow about the passing of the Annexe era, if indeed they would ever feel sorrow. When they were over there all their thoughts were set upon getting out and now that they had made it, they were not at all sure what they expected. None of them had thought it right through carefully but at the same time every single one of them was absolutely convinced that in 'the main' things would be much better, although early signs had not confirmed that.

One thing that was certain was that their Annexe period was over. Already it was a thing of the past. Something from another time and, it almost felt, another place. Ginger didn't really miss the Annexe. He just accepted it as part of his life.

A chapter that was now closed. Closed forever.

Another thing that always puzzled him was the lack of information. Bumble would never divulge anything that wasn't essential to get them through the immediate next stage of their training. It may have helped to make their young lives a bit more bearable if they had been able to see the overall picture or at least see where each segment of training was leading.

It may have made a difference, who could tell. Anyway they were away from the Annexe now and about to be launched into the routine of the Main Establishment. Retaining lingering thoughts of the past would not help in the least.

But despite the changes that had happened to them in such a short space of time, they were still in the dark. Some things hadn't changed at all.

Why was it nobody was prepared to put them in the picture? Why were they expected to stumble from one happening to the next with usually no more than a few minutes warning?

They didn't know anything about the film show until about half an hour before it started. They didn't know anything about getting cocoa and biscuits first thing each morning until someone had been dispatched to the CMG to fetch them. What was this obsession with secrecy?

Soon they would be going over to the CMG for breakfast. They all knew that. But what would happen after breakfast?

They had no idea.

That information, apparently, was still on the secret list.

It was Thursday and Thursday breakfast was 'Train Smash'.

Strange how most pusser's breakfasts were referred to by a comic nickname. Strange how that kind of learning was easy to absorb. Within a very short time all boys had the alternative names for various breakfasts weighed off.

'Train Smash' was bacon and tinned tomatoes. Thursdays were 'Train Smash' days. Other days had their own offering, it was almost part of tradition.

Another day it would be 'Bangers and Red Lead'—sausage and tinned tomatoes; another would be 'Cowboy'—bacon and beans. 'Cackle Berries' were hard boiled eggs, still in their shells.

'Shit on a Raft' was very descriptive because that's what kidneys on fried bread looked like. Also fitting that descriptive train of thought was the more genteel 'Floating Haystacks'. That was the name for Shredded Wheat in milk.

The nearest they came to a nautical theme was 'Yellow Peril'. That was smoked haddock. So much for trying to be topical though, no-one like the rotten stuff.

Sunday breakfast was always traditional egg and bacon.

It seemed to young Ginger that it was more than likely that every boy who had ever gone through Ganges had all these names and more, imprinted on his brain.

There were many more gastronomic delights, among which was 'Cheese Ush' (macaroni cheese); 'Chinese Wedding Cake' (boiled rice pudding); 'Spotted Dick' (duff with currants) and 'Niggers in the Snow' (boiled rice with currants).

Some even had variations that depended on what part of the country they originated.

Like 'Tiddley Oggies', which were a kind of a meat and vegetable pasty— cum—pie kind of thing that had it's origins down in the West Country. Unfortunately its fame had spread to such an extent that forms of it were made all over the place. Everybody cooked them but not everybody, including Ganges cooks, got them right. Word was from boys who had already been home on leave, that they made great ammunition for throwing out of train windows.

A universal favourite was 'Mashed Monkey' or 'Dog'. Both terms were equally popular for the great stand-by, corned beef. Corned 'Dog' could be served cold, or hot with chips or mash, or floured and called fritters, or even chopped up and slung into 'Tiddley Oggies'.

Every Ganges boy had all these names and descriptions weighed off to perfection. If they held examinations for alternative names for food, every boy would have been top of the class. Unfortunately there was no such subject on the agenda and the boys were obliged to struggle and sweat over such unnecessary things as clove hitches, sheet bends and which was port or starboard.

They couldn't be expected to remember every little detail

Leverett had shown them the way to the dining hall once and now they were old hands at negotiating the way, thanks mainly to that chap from 48 mess. Now, three meals later, the old hands were blazing a trail to the their first breakfast with all the confidence that comes with experience.

It was essential to get rid of that 'nozzers' tag as quickly as possible. Although they were new boys and would remain so for some time, at least until the next batch came over in six weeks time, it was not necessary to broadcast the fact.

The first couple of times they had gone to the CMC in a large group, but now with the dawning of a new day, they were making a point of just drifting over in twos and threes.

They had to make their mark. They had something to prove, if only to each other. They'd been and seen and done it all before. They were as good as anybody else. After all by dinner time they would have lots of experience under their belts. Twenty four hours worth of experience.

Back in the mess after breakfast a buzz of excitement filled the air. It started as soon as the first few of them returned from breakfast and seemed to grow as more and more came in.

The atmosphere wasn't anything like as strong as it was when they learned they had to climb the mast, a few weeks back, but there was certainly excitement in the place. They were still in the dark as far as the programme was concerned, but the excitement was real enough. It was probably triggered by speculation as much as anything; a journey into the unknown was bound to have some effect on them in some way. It manifested itself as this nervous, niggling excitement.

'I wonder if they have morning Divisions over here, like they did in the Annexe,' asked Daisy quite suddenly out of the blue.

Daisy was a small, slight, young looking, fresh-faced lad. They were all young but Daisy stood out because of his youthful looks.

PO Jury had christened him Daisy almost from the moment he had first set eyes on him in 49 mess. Maybe there was something effeminate about him that Jury had noticed, who could tell. Daisy was a friendly chap and he had accepted his new name in the spirit that it was intended. There was no hidden under tones or anything nasty about it at all.

'Leave off, Daisy,' said Ray Leeward, replying to Daisy's question. 'We've finished with all that Divisions business now. There won't be any more of that old carry on over here. The Annexe was for teaching us about that sort of thing. Now we're over here we shall be busy learning about ships and things. We passed our parade drill when they brought the band over for our final march past. If we hadn't passed out, we would have been back classed.'

That seemed logical enough and there were murmurs of agreement from the boys.

'Well, you'd have thought someone would have told us, wouldn't you,' said Mick Southern. 'At least old Bumble used to tell us what to do.'

Mick was a tall chap with a pronounced Midlands accent. He suffered from acne, which gave his face a permanent red flushed look. He'd been a bit on the quiet side in the Annexe and somewhat accident prone. If there was anything to knock over, Mick was the one that usually obliged.

Ginger had got to know Mick early on and, on the face of it they didn't seem to have much in common. But that for reasons that can best be described as 'just happening', they got on pretty well together and occasionally sought out each others company.

Although he had known Mick was coming to Hawke with him, Ginger was surprised to hear him speak up. It wasn't that he didn't think Mick would speak up, it was simply that he had forgotten all about him. He hadn't given his old mate a thought all day yesterday and now that he'd seen him he was glad they were together again.

'Whatcha Mick,' he said .

'Hello mate,' replied the tall Midlander, a mixture of surprise and delight registering on his face.

'I'd forgotten all about you,' they both blurted out together.

Nervous self-conscious laughter helped to patch over the mild embarrassment they both felt at having said the same thing.

'Where's your bed then?' asked Ginger. He was standing next to his bed. Mick's question remained unasked, the answer was obvious.

'Over the other side, down there,' he said indicating further down into the mess and at the same time leading Ginger by an arm on the shoulder. He allowed Mick to steer him down the mess; he was pleased to see his old pal again and now he was being invited to 'visit'.

Ganges boys were very possessive about their little bit of space that held their bed and locker. It was their own little domain. They had no privacy at all in Ganges—even the toilets had no doors on them—but their own little bit of bed space was treated like private territory. It had never been said in so many words, or at least not in their time, but everyone respected that quaint little custom. Now Mick was inviting him to visit with all the dignity that wouldn't have been out of place if he had been showing him round his brand new house.

Despite there being no chairs in 49 mess the boys were not allowed to sit on their beds during the day. All blankets had to be folded up in a certain manner with the blue bedspread and pillow on top and that was the way they had to remain all day.

Nevertheless the boys did sit on their beds when the instructors were not about, but always with one eye on the door. Another part of the custom was never to sit on anyone else's bed without an invitation to do so. Such invitations were rarely extended.

Mick steered Ginger to a bed down on the right hand side and sat down on it, patting the mattress alongside him, indicating that he should do the same.

'What do you think is happening then,' Ginger asked. His pal looked blank.

'I'm sure someone will tell us soon,' he replied. His tone suggested that he wasn't too sure. 'I shouldn't think there'll be any more Divisions though. We've been through that stuff and it'll be time to move on to something new.'

Mick had a good mind and usually his thinking was logical and precise. Another time though, he would appear unbelievably thick. What he had just said made perfect sense. Today must be one of his good days.

Suddenly a thought struck Ginger.

'Listen you lot,' he said, jumping to his feet. 'I've just remembered. Today is Thursday. I don't know about over here but in the Annexe Thursday was clean clothes day. I think we'd better put clean No. 8s on just in case.'

'That's daft,' said a dark haired Welsh boy. 'They won't expect us to change in mid week over here. No, we're OK like we are. If we had to change someone would have said so.'

'Yeh, he's got a point. If they wanted us to change into clean gear, someone would have said so. Yeh, he's right. We won't need to change mid week any more,' Ray Leeward was adding his two pen'orth.

'Well, I'm for changing anyway,' said Dereham, speaking for the first time since breakfast. Dereham wasn't one of the worlds great thinkers, but he had bulk on his side and that often helped him make his point.

Then Mick joined in saying that to change was the answer.

'Well I'm going to change anyway,' said Dereham.

'Yah, me too,' agreed Mick.

'And me,' confirmed another voice—then another.

'If one gets changed then we'll all have to get changed,' said Daisy, 'right or wrong we'll all have to be the same.'

'Then change it is,' said Ginger. He had been all for changing. It was no hardship, they'd done it twice a week so far and if it wasn't necessary over here then at least they'd all look smart for their first full day and that might help to keep Leverett and Bachelor off their backs for a while.

'OK then, everybody change into clean and pressed number eights,' commanded Dereham at the top of his voice. He had taken it upon himself to give the orders. It was easy making decisions after they had already been made. Dereham had the weight and the muscle; it was easy for him to throw his weight about. He wasn't hampered by a brain.

PO Jury entered the mess and walked up and down without saying a word, as if waiting for something to happen. Then, right on cue, like an answer to his silent prayer, the Tannoy buzzed into life.

'Out pipes. Boys muster on the parade ground for Daily Divisions.'

Daily Divisions. So they did have Divisions every morning just the same over here. At least that put an end to the speculation.

Another thought suddenly struck Ginger. Back in the Annexe, that afternoon when he was talking to Derek Squires, the chap from Anson, Derek had mentioned being guard class after they had been out repairing sea walls and mopping up after the floods.

He had said that his class had to work all weekend to get their drill perfected so that they could perform at daily Divisions.

Of course, it all came back now, now that it was too late. If only he had remembered it would have solved that will—we, won't—we agonising that they had just been going through..

PO Jury was clanking a stick about inside the empty dustbin.

'Come on then, you heard it...down below then. Whatcha waiting for.'

Descending the stairs they each offered up a silent prayer of thanks that the vote had gone in favour of changing.

Chapter 9

Down below was a hive of activity. As he came out of the mess door he was met by a sea of swirling bodies. All of Hawke Division was there. The colonnade was packed to overflowing. Further to the left he could see that the boys from the other Divisions had congregated in front of Collingwood Block.

Collingwood was to the South of Hawke and turned at right angles. Hawke messes were on an East–West line; Collingwood, the red brick buildings, ran North–South. They were set further back than the Hawke colonnade and this created a space, the length of the nearest mess and to the edge of the parade ground. The space was bordered by Hawke to the North and the back of Benbow to the South.

Whether it was designed that way or if it was simply coincidence, no-one only the original planners and the architects would know. But it made an ideal alcove for boys to muster in, prior to being called to daily Divisions.

The parade ground was empty, apart from a few GIs strutting about and looking very important, in the way that all Gunnery Instructors had of looking important.

Suddenly everything went quiet. The low hubbub of voices and the shuffling of feet stopped abruptly as a fat chief GI in the centre of the parade ground bellowed one single word , 'PARADE'.

That man had a powerful voice and his command carried with it all the impact of an exploding bomb. The boys heard him; everybody heard him. Even the people down in the village must have heard him.

His next outburst was just as explosive.

'Markers—Take post.'

At this shout, boys ran on to the parade. The boys from 49 mess didn't know what was going on; nobody had mentioned anything about this. They were the markers for each mess. How they knew where to go was a mystery. Ginger was just glad that it wasn't him and he didn't have to do it.

'That's where we are, look. Look, over there,' whispered Daisy.

They followed the line where Daisy was looking and out there on his spot, was Shavers, one of the boys from 49 mess. Shavers was tall and thin, an ideal corner man for Divisions. How he got there they didn't know. Jury must have told him what to do and where to go.

After a few seconds there was silence once again as the markers stopped shuffling about on their marks and stood still. Then the fat chief GI's voice boomed out again.

'Divisions—Fall in.'

At this command the place once again became a hive of activity as almost two thousand boys raced for positions alongside their respective markers. They knew more or less what to do, courtesy of the Annexe. The only real difference was that this time there seemed to be a lot more urgency and there was a lot more boys involved.

The nozzers first Divisions in the main was under way.

They had met Cassidy, the DO, when he had bumbled his way through what passed as his 'welcome to Hawke' speech but only that once. All the other DOs were out there, but Cassidy was nowhere to be seen. Word from the older hands from the other messes was that he rarely put in an appearance.

He was obliged to show his face on Sunday Divisions apparently, plus an occasional daily Divisions when Hawke were duty Division. Today didn't appear to be one of those days.

But Batchelor, the second in command, was a different story altogether. He was always around. At odd times during the day, early morning or late at night he would suddenly appear. They had learned already that they were never going to be safe from him. He revelled in being nasty and making the boys lives as uncomfortable as possible.

Cassidy always seemed to be faintly embarrassed, as if there was somewhere he would rather be. Beneath his bumbling, childlike bashfulness though, they were warned he had a mean streak, so none of them felt any sympathy for him.

Who cared about him anyway. He was a pilot and maybe he didn't want to be in charge of two hundred and fifty boys. They were all held there against their will, so why should he be any different. At least he could go out at nights and weekends.

They were told that he rarely, if ever, spoke to the boys directly. He had a way of talking about them as if they incapable of understanding.

'Er, Petty Officer, this boy has a lace undone ....' or 'Have this boy report to my office, Petty Officer.'

He never addressed Jury or Leverett by name, it was always 'Petty Officer.'

Ginger never had the misfortune to be singled out by him, but on their first Sunday Divisions that misfortune almost befell him.

49 mess were fell in for inspection, as was customary and Cassidy was inspecting his own Division for a change. The captain only inspected one Division each time and this wasn't Hawke's turn. Along came Cassidy, followed by Batchelor, followed by PO Jury. They were followed by the class leader-boy bringing up the rear. This, they had been told was standard procedure.

Cassidy was striding along fairly quickly, just casting an eye over the assembled boys but as he drew level with Ginger, something caught his attention. He stopped directly in front of him and just stood there staring for what, under the circumstances, seemed a very long time. His eyes wandered up and down, from the polished boots to the top of the white blancoed hat, then—'Take this boys name, Petty Officer.'

Jury, caught unawares, pushed past Batchelor and completely misread where Cassidy was looking.

'Certainly sir. This is Dereham,' he said. Something must have been wrong but Cassidy didn't elaborate and Jury made no attempt to explore the matter any further.

Dereham was standing to attention next to Ginger. Cassidy wasn't looking at him but luckily he didn't know their names. He made no comment.

Then, after a few more seconds glaring, his expression changed, as if he had lost the thread of his thinking. At the same time he realised he was holding up the procession. His face took on that embarrassed expression of his and he mumbled, as much to himself as anything.

Turning to continue along the remainder of the rank, he said over his shoulder: 'Dereham. Umm, yes. Er, well done Dereham.'

Dereham was puzzled; Ginger was in the clear and no-one ever did learn what that little episode was all about.

As always Batchelor was in close attendance. He was shorter than PO Jury and as Jury had pushed in front of him, he was unable to see properly or hear what was going on. The urgency to get on with Divisions and the march past, forestalled any prying from him. If time had allowed he could have been relied upon to hold a full scale enquiry on the spot.

Batchelor was like that. It was his nature. The boys sometimes felt that he couldn't help himself. He was nasty and quite often downright evil. No-one liked him. They always knew where they stood with Batchelor. Whatever the occasion, whatever the circumstances, if he was involved then, automatically, they were in the wrong.

That meant that they could look forward to some form of punishment— usually dished out by him personally.

Even just to speak to him, not that any of them did that willingly, meant going through a minor ordeal.

He would expect them to double over to him and, of course, they wouldn't have doubled correctly. They would be expected to salute him and— naturally—the salute wouldn't be exactly correct and just standing still would bring forth—'That's not the way to stand to attention.'

He would go to incredible lengths just to try to catch some boy doing something he was not supposed to be doing, even if it meant making something up.

However small the offence, or the alleged offence, it would command his full wrath. His anger just had to be an act put on to satisfy his lust for power and authority. They were all afraid of him so his tirades went unreported. There was nothing to report in any case because he knew how to cover himself.

The boys also knew how to cover him. Six feet of soil sounded good.

Batchelor was at his happiest when he could get a squad of boys together for extra drill, they had to have done something really wrong for him to get his full enjoyment though. It was not so much fun just drilling a squad of boys; that was ordinary, everybody did that all the time. He wanted to drill boys as a form of punishment. That way he could let all his temper and nastiness out without anyone suspecting he was on one of his ego trips.

One afternoon his frustrations must have got the better of him. His need for an ego boost must have outweighed everything else, causing him to throw caution to the wind in his quest for power. But even then, with everything going for him and nothing in the boys favour, he still managed to get all his own way in his lust to dominate.

On this particular day Ginger hadn't been selected to play in the game of cricket the boys of 49 mess had organised for the afternoon. It was early days and they hadn't got involved into the mainstream sports activity yet so they had sorted out a game between themselves, one class against the other. As he wasn't playing he was in no hurry to get to the sports field and that proved to be his undoing.

There will be plenty of time to put in an appearance later, he thought. The first order of business was to keep well out of everyone's way for at least an hour.

They had all been gone for several minutes when he decided to amble down. They hadn't wanted him to play cricket and he wasn't keen enough to bother about watching.

As he stepped out of the mess door, he caught Batchelor's attention. 'That boy there.'

Batchelor had a terrible nasal growl. How he came to have such a pronounced accent was a mystery to the boys. Maybe he was a German. Maybe he had been captured somewhere and had managed to grovel his way into changing sides. That would suit his underhanded ways a treat. But at the same time his voice was powerful. Too powerful to ignore.

'Report to me.'

Ginger had always thought that was a silly thing to say. They all said it, but what did it actually mean. Report. Report what? Why didn't they just say 'come here', after all that is what they meant by that ridiculous phrase.

Batchelor was on the edge of the parade ground, about twenty yards away. He had three boys from 49 mess in front of him; the boys were in sports rig.

Without knowing how they got there, Ginger knew exactly why they were there. Batchelor was having one of his surges of power.

Mac, the blond boy from London, was nearest to where Ginger was standing. JF was next to him and Hyphen-Wotsit was on the other end. Hyphen-Thingy was a small fat chap. He had a dark complexion and straight black hair. They didn't get much money, five bob a week to be precise, but he must have spent most of his on Brylcream; his hair—what there was of it—was always neatly combed and slicked down. He had a double barrelled name and the boys had latched onto it right from the start.

Ginger had first referred to him as Hyphen-Wotsit when they were in the Annexe and the name was quickly picked up by the others. When they realised that he wasn't going to retaliate the name became widespread.

He was a quiet chap. He never joined in anything and he rarely spoke unless someone spoke to him first. He certainly never spoke out, not even in his own defence. He was a friendly boy and as he didn't bite back the joke soon fell flat. Soon he was accepted as 'Hyfe' or 'Dot', as in Dot—Dash—Dot.

Today Batchelor had them on the parade ground. Ginger guessed why. It wasn't a guess, it was a certainty and if he didn't watch his step he would be joining them.

He stood still, looking at Batchelor. The officer was staring back. Ginger knew that Batchelor expected to be obeyed immediately; he knew that he was unlikely to repeat the order and that every extra second it took to report to him would make matters worse. He was caught and they both knew it. His only chance was to brazen it out.

He ran across the few yards that separated them and stood to attention.

'What are you doing boy?'

'Jus' on my way to the sports field, sir,' he lied.

'Why didn't you go when the rest did?'

'I was making my kit neat and tidy sir,' he replied, still lying.

He looked the officer straight in the eye. He might as well make a fight of it, he was caught anyway.

'I see. Who gave you permission to stay behind?'

Ah. Batchelor had won the first point. It was no good saying Jury or Leverett had given him permission because Batchelor would ask them.

'No-one sir,' he conceded, feeling a bit sheepish. That straight in the eye look hadn't worked. He was too nervous to try it again.

He was planning to skive off somewhere for an hour or so, but he had run into Batchelor before his plan had even got under way. He should have known Batchelor would be there to catch him. Batchelor was always there.

The thin ringer clasped his hands behind his back and slowly looked Ginger up and down, clicking his heels together as he did so.

He didn't say a word but Ginger was beginning to tremble. Slowly and deliberately he walked all the way round him, his hands still clasped behind his back. He could feel those evil eyes boring into the back of his head, he stood still not daring to move. Batchelor was horrible but there was something about him that suggested he was enjoying this.

There had to be something wrong. Maybe a lace was undone .... maybe his stockings were not pulled up correctly .... maybe his shorts were not clean enough .... maybe he needed a haircut ....

By the time he had completed his circuit and they were face to face again, Batchelor's face had darkened. He never registered anything but a scowl but was there the merest hint of disappointment showing.

Apparently he could find nothing wrong but that was not going to stop him.

'Why are you not with the rest of your class?'

That deep nasal German accent was getting the full treatment; it seemed to be more pronounced when he was on one of his sadistic ego trips.

'I told you sir. I had to finish off my kit.'

There was no alternative, he had to try to brazen it out although his story wasn't very convincing.

'The rest of your mess are playing cricket today.'

It was a statement rather than a question, but it looked like he was waiting for an answer.

Ginger obliged with one.

'Yes sir.'

'Then why are you not with them?'

'I wasn't picked for the team so I stayed behind for a few minutes to work on my kit sir,' he persisted with his lie.

Working on kit was a good old standby. Everybody used it. It usually brought forth a favourable response and sometimes scored a few points as well.

Batchelor wasn't playing that game. Maybe he'd heard it before.

'When did you last lay out your kit for inspection?'

Oops, careful with that one. The wrong answer here could result in a repeat performance this afternoon.

'This morning sir,' he lied triumphantly.

Batchelor still had his hands clasped behind his back and he was standing still, apart from the occasional click of his heels but something had changed. In a matter of a second his whole attitude was different. The scowl lightened and, if he didn't know better, Ginger could have sworn that for the briefest moment a flicker of a smile graced that snarl hardened mouth.

It was Christmas; it was his birthday and he'd won the football pools all on the same day. He turned about with exaggerated smartness and marched about ten paces to the other end of the line where the other three boys were still standing then, turning about to face Ginger again, he growled his *coup d'état.*

'So, your kit's in perfect order and you're not playing cricket. In other words, you have nothing to do. Perhaps you'd like to join us. Fall in on the end there.'

That was not an invitation. That was an order. Batchelor had won the next point; he had won the contest.

Really, Ginger knew it was a forgone conclusion from the moment he was first spotted. He had tried to brazen it out but it was a 'no-contest' all the way. He'd tried smoke screen tactics and even the old time honoured 'working on my kit' routine, but to no avail. Batchelor would have found something however hard he had wriggled.

It was a one sided contest and he hadn't been dealt any winning cards

Batchelor had won. He had some boys that needed extra discipline. He was prepared to take on their punishment personally. Nobody could question his actions now.

What the others had done was never mentioned. Maybe they looked at him when they were going to the sports field, maybe they were talking or not walking quickly enough. Maybe the sky was too blue—who could tell. It didn't matter what they had done, or for that matter what they hadn't done. Batchelor had a squad and now he could act out his little fantasy with impunity.

He made them march up and down while he shouted various orders at them.

'Right turn .... left turn .... about turn.'

Each time they executed his latest command he would bend down alongside them watching every move they made with their feet; sometimes he got on his knees for a closer look. He expected perfection; he wanted absolute precision.

After almost every manoeuvre he would call them to a halt and make them go over it again by numbers, calling out the numbers as they went.

'When I say feet at forty-five degrees to each other, that's what I expect to see,' he growled.

He wasn't addressing anyone in particular or referring to any specific incident. He was drunk with power.

He even went to the extent of grabbing one of JF's legs, lifting it up and putting it down again where he wanted it to be, a mere fraction of an inch from where it was before. JF, caught unawares by this sudden and unexpected movement, grabbed hold of Mac's shoulder for a bit of support and to save himself losing balance. Batchelor didn't notice that little incident; he was so engrossed down there with JF's feet that he missed a golden opportunity to have them do at least four laps of the parade ground.

His favourite move was the 'about turn' whilst on the march. He made them go through that more than anything else. He had them march away about a dozen paces and then turn about and back about the same distance and then turn about again, over and over.

Each time he ran with them and bent down waiting for them to arrive, so he could watch their feet more closely.

'Abarrrr Huh,' he would blast down through his nose each time, followed by: 'Check—Two—Three—Four—Left.'

They all knew exactly how to march and how to turn, they'd been doing very little else for the past six weeks in the Annexe. Batchelor wasn't teaching them anything, he was just playing out his own fantasies.

'That's better, much better,' he would say after every move, 'but it's not still quite how I like to see it done.'

Of course not. They all knew that. If they were the best drill squad in the world it still wouldn't be right until his ego was satisfied.

Even Hyfe was getting fed up with it. Little Hyfe, who wouldn't say boo to a goose.

Batchelor had been pulling his legs about and giving him a private lesson on the end of the line, when suddenly Hyfe could take no more.

'Well that's the way our instructor in the Annexe taught us sir 'an he said it was all right,' he blurted out more from frustration than bravery. Unfortunately he picked the wrong person to have a bravery attack against.

Batchelor exploded right in his face.

'I didn't give you permission to speak, boy. I don't want to know what your instructor told you. This is the way I expect to see things done. When you're on my parade you will do things the way I want them done.'

Hyfe's face took on a distinct crestfallen look at that and he instantly decided discretion was better than any further comment on the subject.

After a while the about turn was performed satisfactorily. Either that or Batchelor decided that it wasn't going to get any better and they moved on to learning how to stand at ease properly, or at least properly the Batchelor way.

The four of them stood there like statues. Feet apart, hands behind the back, fingers outstretched and pointing downward, palms outward. They knew how to do it. But naturally it was not good enough for Batchelor.

'Shoulders back. Back lad, back,' he shouted grabbing Ginger from behind and pulling his shoulder back even further. He was nearly off balance but he wasn't going to chance saying anything.

'Shoulders back,' was an expression he used a lot.

Another stupid order he appeared to have imprinted on his brain was 'Head up and tuck your chin down.'

No normal person could possible hold their head up and tuck their chin down at the same time, but that's what Batchelor expected them to do.

However the fun had gone out of his little jaunt now. His ego had been fed and the urgency had gone out of his voice. The boys knew it was nearly at an end.

They had been standing at ease for quite a while, with Batchelor out of sight behind them when suddenly he said, his tone softer and almost patronising—'That's better, much better. That's how I expect to see you every time you're on my parade.'

Then, walking round to the front and facing them, he growled

'Right fall out and carry on to the sports field and don't forget what you've been taught.'

With those words he marched away, leaving them standing there. He'd had enough. Their ordeal was over.

The whole episode had been an ego trip for him. There was no other explanation. He wanted someone to bully and nozzers not long over from the Annexe were ideal candidates. They were afraid to say anything and he could have all his own way.

He could have had the rest of the day off and been sitting in the officers wardroom but instead he was prepared to put himself out and make some boys lives a misery.

After his bullying on their first afternoon and now this, the boys realised they had Batchelor to contend with as well as Leverett. Leverett was nasty but Batchelor was worse than nasty—he was evil. Reflecting back, they were beginning to wonder if the main was all they had convinced themselves it was. Maybe it wasn't Utopia after all.

Whatever made them believe that Utopia was over this side of the road. So far this side had been harder and a lot more miserable. The Annexe was hard. It had to be. There was a lot to cram into six weeks, they appreciated that fact now they were over here. But compared to what had happened to them in the recent past, back across the road was like a holiday camp.

Coming over to the main establishment was like rolling out of a feather bed because of a small uncomfortable lump only to land with a crash onto a cold concrete floor.

The routine was hard; the regime was hard. Then, to make matters worse they had two divisional officers who didn't like boys.

Chapter 10

Ginger was not what the Navy called a 'proficient swimmer', or in other words he had so far failed to pass his swimming test. It was nothing to do with not wanting to because it was in his best interests to learn to swim and to do so as quickly as possible.

But after that one can-they-can't-they session when they were marched over from the Annexe, the subject was not mentioned again. Not until they got over to the main permanently that is—and then things took on a new-found urgency.

All the boys that had passed when they came over that first time were sitting pretty because they were not required to go near the pool any more for a while unless they wanted to do so in their free time. Unlike Ginger. Until service papers were marked PST (passed swimming test) and signed by the divisional officer, there was that extra unpleasant task of Backward Swimmers Class to contend with.

The Backward Swimmers Class was extra instruction in the swimming bath, to be undertaken in the non-swimmers free time. There was very little 'free time' to begin with and now the bath's PTIs would ensure there would be even less until the non-swimmers could convince them otherwise.

When 'Backward Swimmers' was first mentioned he naively imagined someone teaching them how to swim backwards. Quite what that would accomplish he couldn't figure out but he reasoned with all his experience gained from a few weeks in the Annexe, that it must be the Navy way.

With all the cack-handed, back to front things the Navy insisted upon, maybe this one had a bit of logic attached to it. Maybe in a shipwreck for example, swimming backwards could get you out of trouble.

But when it came time for his first lesson he was relieved that he hadn't enlightened anyone with that line of reasoning. Backward swimmers class had nothing to do with advanced swimming techniques, or shipwrecks either for that matter.

PO Jury was the one to bring the subject up again when one evening after tea he announced: All those who have not passed their swimming test, stay behind. Remainder fall in outside.'

Where the others were going he didn't mention and Ginger didn't really care, his mind was already on the ordeal by water that lay ahead. Although he hadn't given it any thought until now he guessed that this time the trip wouldn't be quite as easy as it was last time he was in the baths. That time all he had to do was sit and watch

At the poolside everything was just as he remembered it, except this time there was none of the hustle and bustle of everyone trying to impress everyone else.

This time none of them wanted to draw attention to themselves They were all in the same boat—in a manner of speaking—this time none of them could swim. There was a distinct feeling of trepidation in the air that seemed to envelope them all like a cloud.

Backward swimmers from all divisions were there. Although they had all been in the Annexe together, most of them were strangers. They had come from all corners of Ganges; different divisions; different messes; different branches. Now they were drawn together by a common bond: the inability to swim. They had joined the fellowship of Backward Swimmers.

On the way over and while they were getting undressed Ginger had visions of being pushed in at the deep end with a 'swim—or—drown' ultimatum from some loud, muscle-bound PTI, but when they were all inside he was pleasantly surprise to find their PTI for the session was a quietly spoken chap who genuinely wanted to teach young lads how to swim.

This time they were allowed to wear a slip, exactly the same kind as those in Chalkie Whites washhouse back in the Annexe. The slips brought back memories and he guessed that the others were having similar thoughts. But any such thoughts were short lived and the quiet voice of their instructor soon exorcised Chalkie White from their minds.

There was none of the awkward shuffling together and congregating together in an embarrassed heap like there was last time they were at the poolside. This time they'd got a bit of service time under their belts and although that air of not knowing what to expect was nagging them a bit, they had all been there before and they knew more or less what lay in store for them.

PO Jury brought the 49 mess boys over but by the time they had got undressed he and the other divisions instructors had gone.

'Right then, now you've got your slips on get up in the pens and sit down.'

That was the voice of the duty PTI. Now they were on their own he wanted to be getting on with things.

He took them by surprise. Ginger felt sure they would be dispatched up to the deep end and forced to jump in or get pushed in, accompanied by that old sin—or—swim routine. That thinking was courtesy of the 'knowledgeables' back home who had been very free with their advice. Even his father, who had never been anywhere or done anything, taunted: ' The Navy won't have any truck with sailors that can't swim.'

As Ginger made his way up the few steps and sat down in the pen with the others, those words were echoing around in his head.

'They'll chuck you in the deep end and then you'll either sink or swim.'

They didn't 'chuck him in' at all and when he did make it into the water it was at the shallow end. After about half an hour of being shown and practising the leg movements for the breast stroke while sitting on the seats in the pen, the PTI introduced them to the water where the remainder of the period was taken up holding the side and kicking their legs in the prescribed manner. After that the swimming pool and the water lost its formidable feel and through a mixture of fear and necessity they were all finished with Backward Swimmers classes long before the next batch of nozzers joined 'the main'.

The combination of fear at being shouted at and ridiculed by Leverett or Batchelor and the necessity to pass as quickly as possible, because swimming instruction took place on picture show nights and there would be no 'Good old Fred' until those papers were signed PST, was enough incentive to turn the non-swimmers of 49 mess into little Johnny Weismullers in record time.

As each individual progressed so he was tested. Which meant those nearly up to standard took the test after only a couple of sessions.

Ginger didn't even have the basics. He had to start from scratch but he soon cottoned on that it was in his best interests to learn as quickly as possible. Allowing swimming instruction to encroach into their meagre amount of free time coupled with the fact that there would be no picture show until he had passed, was a great incentive and after a matter of only about three weeks he felt brave enough to suggest that he might be ready to take the test.

The chief in charge didn't look particularly impressed and raised a quizzical eyebrow in the direction of the duty PTI. By coincidence the duty man was the fair haired chap who had taken them for their first lesson. He agreed.

Whether he was in a generous mood, whether he hadn't been paying attention or whether he just didn't want to embarrass himself in front of the chief by saying he didn't know, was hard to figure out. But whatever his reasons, he agreed and Ginger was granted a test on the spot which he managed to splutter and splash his way through.

After swimming about in a soggy white duck suit and trying to keep his head above water for what seemed like an eternity, with invisible hands attaching lead weights on him at every stroke, the duty PTI caught his eye and beckoned him to the side. As he reached the side and gratefully grabbed hold, the duty man was joined by the chief.

'Right then. Well done lad. Out of that wet gear and dry off.'

Those few words from the chief were the kindest that anyone had spoken to him since he stepped off that bus in the Annexe on his first afternoon. He had passed.

Despite what his dad had said, the country boy who couldn't swim had passed the Navy swimming test. He was jubilant; he was no longer a Backward Swimmer and now he could take his place with the others to watch Tom and Jerry at all future picture shows.

But if he thought passing the swimming test heralded the end of his problems, he was sadly mistaken. He was the only one that felt any jubilation. There was no spontaneous applause, no back slapping, no congratulatory handshakes, not even a mumbled 'well done'. It was just another obstacle mounted along the obstacle strewn path of his new career.

He had learned to march; he'd learned how to make his bed; he'd learned how to put his best suit on unaided; he'd learned how to climb that rotten mast—and now he'd learned how to swim. But despite his achievement it turned out to be just another unmarked milestone; simply another notch toward the quota of notches required to allow him to pass out of the place for good some long way into the future.

He was disappointed that no-one had recognised his efforts. He felt that at least one person from 49 mess would have congratulated him. Even the Divisional Officer made no concession toward congratulation either by word or nod and even signed the papers in his absence, although he had been very forthright in telling them how 'backward swimmers let the side down' only a week or two earlier.

In a strange kind of way that was Ganges. In some kind of unspoken—and perhaps even unrealised—way, they were not geared to applauding individual achievements.

Naturally there were the frontrunners, the kind who were always striving to get themselves noticed and, of course, there was the occasional outstanding sportsman. Boxing or swimming for example where once in a while someone would emerge head and shoulders above everyone else. But even so it was still considered a team effort, although most of the effort—or at least the results—came from the one team member.

So really, although he didn't realise it, the lack of congratulations was just par for the course as far as the Ganges mentality was concerned.

Cassidy, the Divisional Officer, had laboured the point about 'letting the side down' only a few short weeks ago but that was simply the Ganges mentality at work. The 'side' that he referred to was that indefinable team thing. Team, in this case, meant class and the class, as far as swimming was concerned in his eyes, couldn't be a complete 'team' while there were still stragglers. Backward Swimmers as he had told them, were stragglers and stragglers let the side down.

So passing the swimming test, momentous achievement that it was, was simply doing what was expected of him in not letting the side down any longer.

Nevertheless, even in his isolation Ginger had a warm glow. He had achieved something that was all his own work. He could now take his place at all future picture shows and he had proved his father wrong. He felt good.

Chapter 11

Ganges regime was hard, some might say brutal. Some might even say barbaric and on occasion, focusing on isolated incidents, they would be correct.

There were of course moments of humanity. Like the time, for example, when a boy getting his prepared for his final kit inspection, had a tin of paint knocked over his best suit trousers and his mess instructor was out in the Covered Way doing his best to help him clean it off.

But such moments were few and far between. The moments of inhumanity outweighed anything to the contrary by a large margin. Man's inhumanity to man is as old as life itself; there has always been the oppressors and the oppressed. In that league table Ganges must have come very close to the top of that table.

Leverett was their seamanship instructor. Seamanship was his business and from what the boys could tell, he was pretty good at his business.

In the classrooms he was a very competent teacher but outside he was never one for explaining things. He knew what he was doing and he didn't care what anyone else thought. With him it was usually march somewhere and find out where when you get there. There was no reasoning with the man. His concession to reason was very much his own personal approach.

'Stop cackling your fat. Pay attention; do as you're told and don't ask questions.'

Yes, Ganges regime certainly was hard to say the very least.

Tucked into the break of the Long Covered way, behind the old cookhouse, was the Seamanship Block. It was in the space created by the cookhouse but facing the opposite direction, so that the front was facing toward the sick bay buildings. The entrance door, up about four steps off the road, was just a few yards from the top of Laundry Hill.

They'd had a few sessions inside the Seamanship Block, in various classrooms, to learn the theory of using oars in cutters and whalers, how to put up sails and a bit of basic rule of the road—which was what the Navy called keeping out of each others way whilst afloat, whether it be with sails, oars or engine power.

Now it was deemed time to get acquainted with the real thing for the first time and so it was that they found themselves down by the river.

No mention had been made of where they would be going or what they would be doing, when Leverett collected them after Divisions and marched them away.

As it was him that had collected them they guessed it was seamanship classes they were heading for. Where they would be going or what they would be doing when they got there would remain a mystery until he was ready to tell them.

By contrast PO Jury wasn't that bad. He would usually explain as much as he thought the boys needed to know. Normally that wasn't a lot, but his little confidences, relayed in his precise clipped 'naval messages' style of speech helped and it gave them a little bit of encouragement. Jury tried to make them feel that they were part of a team.

As far as they were concerned when they were in the Annexe, that river could have been a hundred miles away. They were not even aware there was a river just down the hill. It was outside the gate where they were not allowed to go and even on the odd occasion that they had ventured outside, it was under strict supervision, like the swimming and mast test days and that didn't take them anywhere near the river anyway.

They were quite close on the day they had their first medical. On that hot afternoon they were almost within spitting distance of the river and if they'd had the presence of mind to listen, they would have heard the sounds associated with river traffic in a busy harbour. But they had other things on their mind that day without worrying about rivers. The undressing and getting dressed again outside was a new experience for them, not to mention the frustrations of getting a new serge suit of and on again in the heat, for the first time.

But any ideas they had that being near the river on a warm sunny day was just a myth and that myth was exploded when Leverett introduced them to the delights of the boat jetty.

It was down at the bottom of the infamous Faith, Hope and Charity, three sets of stone steps that led down past the Signal School and Dental Block. They were well aware of those steps having travelled them in both directions, several times and at the double.

The boat jetty was a long L shaped structure that stuck out into the river, with cutters and whalers hoisted up on davits along its length.

Once back under the control of the class instructor after a period away from them, like the school sessions for example, it was not unusual to find that 'We shall double to your next class via Faith, Hope and Charity'—or Laundry Hill—for no other reason than to satisfy some perverse pleasure known only to class instructors.

Ships company and to some extent, PTIs were not too bad. The ones to watch out for were the class instructors and not just those from your own division either. The boys were convinced that these people were bred for one specific purpose—to become a Shotley instructor. They all seemed to have that same sadistic streak to their nature and it appeared that they were chosen to become instructors because of that very quality.

But even in the league table of Shotley instructors Leverett was in a class of his own. In that respect the boys of 49 mess really hit the jackpot when they were assigned to him. He was a hard task master and he probably appeared more so because they all feared him. There was no such thing as a pleasant time if he had anything to do with it.

He enjoyed being down on the river, it appeared to give him some personal satisfaction. He could still make things as difficult as possible for the boys but at the same time enjoy a couple of hours 'messing about in boats'. Even the permanently turned down corners of his mouth managed an occasional smile when they were away in a boat. It didn't matter if it was rowing or sailing, just the fact that they were on the river made Leverett happy.

Unfortunately his happiness wasn't contagious and Ginger experienced none of his euphoria. To him, trips on the river with Leverett spelt lots of hard work nearly always coupled with wet clothes and cold winds.

Boat drill and taking away boats, either under sail or with oars, could be a dangerous business. The heavy mast to be man handled in a rocking boat was no easy matter particularly with an inexperienced crew such as they were. They were not allowed to stand up or move about more than was absolutely necessary and that made it difficult to hump the mast around and get it upright. Even the oars in the cutters were big and cumbersome. They must have weighed nearly as much as some of the smaller boys.

They'd had first hand experience of those oars long before they got near the water though, when Leverett made sure they spent some time in the 'Dry Land Cutter'. This was an old 32 feet long cutter set up near the seamanship block. It was nowhere the river and it stood on a concrete base. The object of it was to familiarise them with the layout of a cutter and see how things worked before they got involved on the river with the real thing.

But Leverett would have none of that. He made them climb in, about a dozen at a time, then he would make them get the oars out and pretend they were rowing along. Without the support of the water to help to take some of the weight, those oars almost outbalanced the boys but he didn't care. One day he made them sit in the boat holding the oars out at right angles until someone collapsed, unable to control that heavy lump of wood any longer.

Thanks to Leverett—and the fear he injected into them—the boys of 49 mess knew how to man and row, raise the mast and hoist sail of a cutter and whaler, long before any of them had been near the river.

Boats were never a pleasant experience for Ginger, although some of the others seemed to enjoy themselves down on the river. It always appeared to be cold and windy, even on the sunny days and, of course Leverett was always there; no experience was ever pleasant if he was involved.

So it triggered a bit of speculation when he announced, before breakfast one morning: 'Sea training today.'

They'd heard the term before, but only in passing and from the more senior classes. None of them had given it much thought. It was self explanatory really. Sea training, or training for sea. What was new about that. Wasn't what they were doing every day.

It was pouring with rain when they made their way over to breakfast and it was still lashing it down as they marched to the boat jetty an hour later.

PO Jury was with them as well so it looked like being some kind of special day. That theory was confirmed when they stopped off outside the CMG to pick up containers of food.

They reached the boat jetty at about 0830 and a motor launch came alongside.

'Right then,' screamed Leverett above the wind and lashing rain. 'Load the gear inboard, get yourselves aboard and standby to cast off.'

By this time some of the more knowledgeables had figured it out and the word quickly spread around the launch.

'We're going on a ship.'

It seemed a logical conclusion to be drawn as they ploughed steadily through the choppy water, particularly when they realised they were heading for a ship anchored further out in the estuary.

Ginger had never seen such a big ship. He had never actually seen a warship of any size before. He didn't know the difference between a merchant ship and a Navy ship in any case, so he certainly didn't know a big ship, as opposed to a small ship, when he saw one unless of course there were two together of different sizes. This one lay in isolation and he didn't have a clue.

As they drew closer he could see the numbers D139 painted in black on the grey ships side. There was a motorboat tied up alongside.

Their motor launch came to a stop beside some wooden steps that were attached to the ship and Leverett soon had the boys scrambling up those steps and onto the ship.

The rain was still lashing down and the wind was cold but at least the ship didn't bounce about like the launch had.

Once they were all safely onboard and the launch had left, they began to huddle round the funnel for a bit of warmth and shelter from the wind and rain. But their little respite was short lived because almost at once the Tannoy burst into life with the Quartermasters pipe: 'All hands—up motorboat'

The motorboat had been deliberately left down so that the boys could gain some first hand knowledge of how to hoist it inboard and secure it for sea. They'd done the theory in the seamanship block and they had raised the cutters and whalers on the boat jetty davits, but this was the real thing. They were on a real ship and about to see a motor boat hoisted for real, just like real sailors.

The only fly in the ointment was that when the Tannoy said 'All Hands', what they actually meant was all boys. Apart from the boats crew around the boat, the only people manning the falls were the residents of 49 mess.

Hoisting the boat wasn't as much fun as they expected it to be. They had jumped to it with boyish enthusiasm but freezing cold water from rain soaked rope falls dribbling over numb fingers and running up inside of oilskin sleeves soon took the edge off the whole proceedings.

Next on the agenda was everybody up to the fo'castle deck to weigh anchor. That wasn't too bad because all the boys had to do was watch while the ships anchor party did the work. Again the boys knew the theory, having seen it done on the model in the seamanship block.

The next bit was even better.

'Everyone back down the ladder and inside, through the door,' ordered Leverett.

They were eager to comply with that order instantly because it meant getting out of the weather and into the warm. They entered into a long passage. By the time the last boy was in and the door closed, Jury and Leverett were gone.

One of the ships Petty Officers was waiting for them. His function was to tell them about the ship.

'This is HMS Obdurate, She is an 'O' class destroyer. She is fitted out for mine laying,' he droned.

He didn't look very interested and Ginger wondered how many times he had gone through this same routine.

The captain is Commander Mentethe, that's M–E–N–T–E–T–H–E,' he continued.

He didn't look as if he cared if they were listening or not. He had been told to relay details of his ship and that was exactly what he was doing.

'The ships length is 345 feet and she has a beam of 35 feet. She has two turbine engines which develop 40,000 horse power. At full load she displaces 2,500 tons,'

He had all the facts in his head, drummed in by continually repeating them to successive classes on their sea training day.

'She has three 4 inch guns, four 2 pounders and three 40 millimetres. She was built in Dumbarton, Scotland in 1942—now, if there are no questions it's stand-easy. The canteen is up there on the right.'

Then, without waiting to see if there were any questions, he turned and walked away along the passage and was lost to sight.

The canteen was a welcome sight; they sold sticky buns. Ganges boys were always hungry and today at sea was no exception.

Someone produced a large kettle of tea and they filled their mugs and ate their buns.

After stand-easy, that same PO returned. There was still no sign of Leverett or Jury.

'Right then you lot listen up,' he began.

He was different; he was not threatening or imposing; he was not a bit like Ganges POs.

'From now until dinner you will break into small groups and look over the ship. Ask questions of anyone you see, if you want to. Right away you go then.'

Then, more quietly, almost as an afterthought, he added: 'It's still pouring down outside, so I'd try to keep down below as much as possible if I were you.'

After dinner the rain had stopped, which was fortunate because straight after dinner the Tannoy cackled—'Away sea boats crew—away sea boats crew.'

Jury appeared from somewhere. It was the first time they had seen him since they had come on board.

'Well, whatcha waiting for. You heard it. Away sea boats crew. Come on then. Move, move, move.'

They scrambled through the door and out on to the upper deck, expecting to see a sea boats display. But instead there was Leverett waiting for them.

'Right then, first five man the boat,' he shouted, chopping of the first five with his arm.

'You five, move it then. Remainder of you lot, man the falls.'

They were expected to man the sea boat, No-one had mentioned that before. No wonder Jury was in such a hurry to get them out.

Ginger had got shoved out of the way when PO Jury ushered them out and that put him near the back. That proved to be a bit of luck because otherwise he would have been one of the first out and almost certainly picked to man the boat. A lifebelt was bobbing about some distance from the ships side, but there was no sign of anyone that had fallen over.

'Well come on then. Man overboard. Get away and retrieve that lifebelt.'

Leverett was in charge of the lifeboat drill. Ginger kept well out of his way.

Those at the front had turned the boat out and the remainder were manning the falls.

'Lower away,' bellowed Leverett.

The boys on the falls walked slowly forward allowing the boat to lower until it was almost in the water, just like they had practiced on the model and experienced on the boat jetty.

'Slip.' Was the next command and the boat was in the water and under way, heading for that lifebelt and the imaginary man overboard.

The boys on the falls had nothing to do now that the weight was off so they watched proceedings from the guardrails until the boat returned.

When it came back the crew re-coupled to the falls and then Leveretts voice rang out again.

'Hoist away.'

At that, the boys on the falls stamped along the iron deck dragging the boat out of the water and back onto its perch.

The sea boat drill took up most of the time until stand-easy, mid afternoon. By the time stand-easy was over they realised how the time had flown and they were back inside the river and heading for home.

There was one more operation to be performed and it was Leverett who ordered—'Everyone back on the fo'castle to watch them drop the anchor.' They knew how that went but it was good to see it done for real.

It went like clockwork, exactly how they had practiced it on the model.

With the anchor down it was time to leave. The motor launch was waiting for them and, as soon as the ship had stopped, it came alongside. A couple of boys had been sent to collect the empty food containers and when they reappeared everyone boarded the launch and they headed back to the boat jetty. The time was nearly 4 o'clock. They'd had a good day out and they were back just in time for tea.

Although the rain had been stopped for quite a time, they wore their oilskins to make the journey back across the river on the open launch. But as soon as they landed on the boat jetty Leverett ordered,

'Off oilskins. Carry them over your arm.'

Usually none of them liked wearing oilskins, they were itchy around the collar and they smelt of old waterproofing, but today they would have liked to have kept them on. They would have looked different; they would have got noticed walking into the CMG wearing oilskins. They could have made a show of taking them off and hanging them up; everyone would have seen them. There would have been no doubt where they had been all day.

In Ganges when it was raining the order of the day would be to wear oilskins. The Tannoy would leave no-one in doubt.

'Dress of the day so-and-so AND oilskins.'

That would not be a suggestion it would be an order, an order that the boys were obliged to obey. On such a day everyone would look the same. But today, now that it was no longer raining they would have looked different.

'Home is the sailor, home from the sea ....'

They felt like sailors, they'd been to sea in a real ship like real sailors and they would have liked everyone to know. But apparently Leverett hadn't grasped the significance of the occasion.

The book said: 'When it rains thou shalt wear oilskins and when it is not raining thou shalt not wear oilskins.'

That is what the book said and as far as Leverett was concerned it was written in stone. PO Jury was with them and he was usually a lot more responsive than Leverett but this time he seemed a bit slow on the uptake as well.

There had been very little of Ganges style routine all day, both instructors had left them alone a lot more than normal and that feeling of well being still prevailed although they were back on *terra firma* once again.

The boys were tired after their day-long excursion and the instructors recognised that fact by allowing them to march up Faith, Hope and Charity rather than the more acceptable method doubling up and down.

Normally it was a case of doubling up and down, just turning about at the top and again at the bottom while the instructor ambled slowly upward, grinning that sadistic grin that only instructors knew how to use to good effect.

The boys all appreciated the slight relaxation of the routine today and that little act of kindness in allowing them to march up that formidable stone stairway.

But it would have been good if they had allowed them to keep those oilskins on a bit longer

Chapter 12

A change is as good as a rest, or so they say.

But the change that the boys of 49 mess were obliged to undertake was most certainly no rest. Particularly as their change came about at a moments notice. They had no inkling that any change was in the pipeline anyway, so it was a complete surprise when PO Jury ordered

'Pack your kitbags, we're moving out.'

Jury was always matter of fact in the way he spoke to them, but at the same time he left them in no doubt. His message was always loud and clear.

'They're going to lay a new deck for us and we've got to move out for a few days while they do it. So everything has to go. Quick as you can then.'

So they found themselves in temporary quarters down under the covered ways. Ginger had never been that way before. They knew about the covered ways. They were in full view from the parade ground and they'd passed close by on the way to the seamanship block but there was no reason for anyone to go down there that didn't actually live there.

The messes were different from Hawke in that they were all single stories. They were all tightly packed side by side, with an identical lot facing them the other side of the covered way.

The covered ways got their name simply because that was what they were. Outside the mess was a wide concrete path that stretched across to the messes facing. The covered ways were in three sections. They each had a roof over them—making them 'covered ways'.

The longest stretch reached all the way from the Quarter Deck down to overlooking the foreshore and the river. As it was the longest bit, it was called imaginatively the Long Covered Way.

A shorter bit ran parallel on the North side and was the Short Covered Way.

The third was a very short section continuing the line from where the Short Covered Way ended. It housed Benbow Division. The two sections were separated by the Recreation Hall. That short bit covered only four messes and covered the area from the Recreation Hall to the Quarter Deck They really excelled themselves by naming that bit Benbow Lane.

They were billeted in the first mess at the top of Benbow Lane and parallel to the parade ground. Unlike Hawke Division, inside the Benbow mess, the messdeck was raised up three or four steps higher than the bathroom and outside door.

A good thing about being down there seemed to be that sometimes people mingled about in the covered ways, talking and just walking about. In Hawke they tended to stay inside their mess. Perhaps it was because it was upstairs and it was too much trouble to walk down or more likely, subconsciously they were probably afraid that if they ventured out they might run into Batchelor.

But whatever the reason the atmosphere seemed a lot more relaxed than it was in Hawke and Ginger took advantage of the situation to wander round and do a bit of exploring.

As it transpired it was a good idea on his part because his pioneering spirit led him directly to witness one of the Ganges time honoured rituals. A ritual they performed upon any boy that was caught swearing in public.

His exploring took him out of their temporary mess and down hill a little way then he turned right into the gap that led to the bath house, which was opposite the old disused cookhouse on the Long Covered Way. Alongside the bath house he stopped for a second deciding which way to go, when an officer came into view.

He was probably a divisional officer from one of the divisions further down. He was walking up toward the Quarter Deck and probably heading for the wardroom which was just beyond.

Ginger stepped back a bit and out of sight; he didn't know this officer and he wasn't about to take any chances. He only had first hand experience of Batchelor and Cassidy from Hawke and, if they were typical, then no officer was to be relied on to mind his own business and leave the boys alone in their spare time. His first priority was to make himself scarce until that officer, whoever he was, had gone past and was out of sight.

He passed close enough for Ginger to see that he had two gold rings on his sleeve, he could almost touch him and at the last second he held his breath in case that officer should hear him breathing. But there was no need. He was intent upon something and was looking straight ahead and even at that distance didn't notice Ginger lurking in the shadows at the side of the bath house as he strode purposefully past.

Only a couple of messes further on another young lad wasn't as fortunate; he came hurtling out of one of the Blake Division messes, which were on the left and very nearly into the arms of the passing officer.

As if it wasn't bad enough to come careering out like that and nearly knocking over someone almost as important as God, the boy had apparently been annoyed about something and was sounding off in a manner guaranteed to make an old salt blush. Realising what he had done, or worse what he had said, he stood there looking very uncomfortable and saluted the officer. At the same time he was twitching about as if he was trying to make up his mind whether to make a dash for freedom

'Stand still, boy,' vibrated under the tin roof.

A look at the two faces left no doubt which of the two had said that. Ginger was still out of sight but he edged forward for a better view.

There then followed a conversation of sorts; a kind of duet for two voices, one very loud and the other barely audible. He didn't need a programme to know who had the loud voice and who had the most dialogue.

The words were not clear. The loud voice rattled its way between the messes and the iron girders of the roof with the boys voice nothing more than a frightened whisper. One thing was certain though, this was no friendly interchange.

Then after a while the conversation came to an end with both participants marching toward the Quarter Deck, the boy in front with his arms swinging up to shoulder height and the officer following behind watching the boys every step.

Ginger stayed where he was until they were gone from sight. He wanted to see what was going on but he didn't want to get caught watching and suffer one of that officers ear bashing.

He'd seen one performance already and that was from a fair distance, but it was still loud enough to make the tin roof rattle and he didn't want to disturb anyone by having that roof rattle again on his account.

By the time he reached the edge of the Quarter Deck they had gone and there was no-one in sight. He figured they must have gone inside the office building. So he found a spot where he could see and at the same time, hopefully, not get seen and stood waiting to see if anything was going to happen.

After a few minutes his patience was rewarded and the boy appeared again, this time a different person was with him. Maybe it was the Quartermaster or the duty RPO. Ginger wasn't keen enough to find out he just stayed in the shadows and watched proceedings.

The officer was nowhere to be seen; the boy and his new escort stopped just outside the office block door.

The boy was carrying a large jar of liquid Teepol and soft soap and some of this liquid he poured into a tin mug. A few words were exchanged then the boy took a mouthful of it. After a few seconds he was told to spit it out, then at the top of his voice he was ordered to shout—'Ahoy, ahoy, ahoy, this will make me a clean mouthed boy.' This process was repeated until the whole mug full of the awful liquid was used.

Ginger stood spellbound, watching that terrible treatment vowing never to swear—or at least to make absolutely sure no-one in authority was listening if he did.

As soon as he felt it was safe to do so he executed a tactical withdrawal. He figured that it was the sensible thing to do because that boy would be coming back that way soon and it was pretty certain that he wouldn't be in a very friendly frame of mind, particularly when he learned that someone had witnessed his humiliation. He retraced his earlier route back to the mess as he beat a hasty retreat before that boy turned up, or indeed before anyone else wanted to look more closely at what he was doing there.

Once back among the familiar faces and the comparative safety of that temporary mess, he got reflecting upon how petty it was to punish people in that barbaric manner for swearing. OK, so swearing wasn't necessary but overall it was harmless and almost everybody did it to some degree. That didn't make it right of course, but by the same token it didn't do any harm.

Nevertheless, the Navy was having none of it and their message was loud and clear: anyone caught swearing would suffer a similar fate to that of the poor unfortunate from Blake Division. Really his crime was simply that of getting caught.

It was early days over in the Annexe when the Navy first made their feelings clear about the business of swearing. One of the very first things they did was to issue everyone with a little white card that contained a list of 'dos' and 'don'ts' for their guidance and, sure enough among such gems as:

'Always treat a woman with courtesy.'

'Never point a gun at anyone, not even in fun,' and one that he always found amusing: 'Never help a woman downward,'—was the 'no swearing' directive.

So they couldn't say they hadn't been warned. How many of them had actually read that little card was a different matter, but they couldn't admit to that either.

Sitting there on his bed, with that soapy gargle episode safely behind him, Ginger recalled that it was the Annexe where he'd had his first demonstration of how seriously the Navy took their no swearing policy.

The two messes that made up each division over there were joined together by one door in the front. That door served both messes. Inside Jellicoe door a passage led off to the left for Jellicoe Two and an identical one led off to the right for Jellicoe One. His first job in his new career with the Royal Navy was to scrub that passage every morning.

He was scrubbing away just inside the door as usual one morning when a boy from Jellicoe One came past shouting for his friend. At the same time the

Divisional Officer just happened to be coming out of his office and overheard the boys shout. Well, not so much overheard as misheard, or at the very least, misunderstood.

The boy's pal was called Puckett and that was what he had shouted. Quite what the DO thought he had said wasn't clear but he moved across the corner of the parade ground at remarkable speed and was outside the Jellicoe door in a flash.

'Come here, that boy. What did you say?'

'I was just calling for my mate sir,' said the boy embarrassed to find the DO suddenly looming over him. He hadn't noticed his rapid approach.

'Tell your instructor that I want you outside the Divisional Office right away.'

The DO was a quietly spoken chap and this was the first time Ginger had heard him speak to any of the boys directly, apart from at the daily Divisions parade. He still didn't raise his voice but his tone was enough to tell Ginger that he meant what he said. The boy got the message too.

He recalled that he quickly mopped up the last little bit of the wooden deck and, grabbing his bucket and scrubber, disappeared back around the corner of the passage and out of sight. He didn't want any of the DO's wrath spilling over onto him.

The remainder of the episode was conducted in the Divisional Office and out of earshot, but it transpired that it took all of the Jellicoe One instructors magic to convince the DO that there was a boy called Puckett. Without the help of that instructor, there's no telling what that innocent boys fate might have been.

In their eagerness to enforce their no swearing policy, they were prepared to go way over the top to ensure that not only was punishment for miscreants harsh, but also that it was brutal enough to deter the fringe element from chancing their arm.

There was another occasion of a similar nature, back in Hawke and now that he was thinking along those lines, that unpleasant episode came back to him as clearly as if it were only yesterday. This time Leverett was involved and that fact alone made it an unpleasant experience.

They were just beginning to feel relaxed and settled in, having been out of the Annexe for a few weeks and Ginger recalled that a group of them were standing around, having a yarn in the middle of the mess, when Leverett walked in. They wasn't doing anything wrong and it was their free time. Quite what Leverett was doing there wasn't clear, but on that particular evening he seemed more relaxed and approachable than usual. He stood listening to the conversation for a while and then he began to join in.

Hesitantly the boys accepted him but with reservations; a few minutes off duty conversation with him wasn't going to make them forget what he was really like. He had his 'hangers-on' of course and, naturally, they 'just happened' to find themselves in close proximity to him, pretending to latch on to his every word.

They had drifted into a kind of circle, most of them standing up with a few sitting on the foot end of the nearest beds. As time progressed the conversation became more relaxed, almost back to where it was before Leverett came in. There wasn't that intense excitement of a huddle that comes after the news of an unpleasant duty or the prospect of a fight; they were not talking about anything specific. It was a spontaneous get together where one subject led to another, with everyone involved having something to say.

In spite of the relaxed atmosphere, Ginger recalled that he still retained some of his natural reserve. Unlike his old pal, JF. Poor old JF got quite carried away with one of his stories and that's how the unpleasantness started.

JF was a midlander, from Nottingham.

He was a slight chap with a rather sorrowful looking face, not unlike Stan Laurel from the old Laurel and Hardy films. His hair stood straight up in the semblance of a crew cut.

This appearance gave a false impression of his personality because he looked nothing like the way his mind worked. He was a friendly enough sort of a chap although he spoke in an aggressive forceful manner. He seemed to be old, far beyond his years and he was always talking about 'a pint of beer' or 'smoking his pipe,' etc. His favourite word appeared to be 'bugger', a word he managed to insert into every sentence that he uttered.

All these things combined put years on him and although he was only a little way into his fifteenth year, his manner and speech were that of someone ten years older. Whether this was something he was working on in an attempt to turn him into a man or whether this was the way he had always been was hard to tell. Either way this was JF, take him or leave him.

Most of the chatter had been good up until this point with everyone laughing and forgetting about Ganges for a while. Standing next to Ginger, JF had the floor as he kept the laughter going with one of his stories. It didn't matter what the tale was really, they were happy and enjoying themselves and ready to laugh at anything. JF was enjoying himself too, laughing along with the rest—and that was his undoing because he wasn't watching his language and a couple of 'buggers' slipped in. He had got away with it twice but he next time was a quiet moment between laughter and Leverett suddenly remembered where he was.

'What did you say?'

The atmosphere became ice cold immediately; all laughter and merriment instantly dead. Leverett had that effect on them. They had given him an opening and he had taken it. Perhaps he thought it would be more fun to bait one of the boys than to join in their fun. Perhaps he thought they would be impressed with him if he made someone squirm. Who could tell what was going on in side that mind of his.

Everyone was standing shock still where they were and looking at him, wondering what would happen next. There wasn't a sound in the place.

Would he send JF to the Quarter Deck to be charged? .... would he make them all double round and round the parade ground? .... would he make them climb the mast in the dark? ....

Leverett looked embarrassed for a second. He had interfered with the boy's free time without reason. He had spoiled their moments of happiness and now, with all eyes on him, he had to save face.

'I said what did you say, boy?'

JF stood bright red in the face and looking most uncomfortable.

'He was swearing sir. You heard him sir. He was swearing.'

The hangers-on left JF no way out. They were in the clear and looking to score a few cheap points with 'sir'.

'So you were swearing were you. You know the penalty for swearing.'

Leverett was back to his old self. How could they have possibly have thought he was being happy with them just a few seconds ago. They all knew better than to trust him, but nevertheless they had lowered their defences.

'Go and get your soap.'

They all knew what was going to happen. He was going to make JF chew a bar of soap.

'Here sir, here's a bar of soap. You can use my soap sir,' one of the hangers-on grovelled, passing a large bar of pussers soap to Leverett

Leverett was in full swing by this time. He had a false smile on his face and he turned round a full circle, willing others to laugh with him; that was his contribution to the fun.

His gaze was met with stony silence.

'Right then lad, you know the penalty for swearing,' he said, offering the bar of soap up to JF's face. 'Take a bite and chew it until I tell you to stop.'

JF stood looking a bit hesitant then slowly he leaned forward eyeing up the soap, probably looking for a small corner to bite off. But Leverett was having none of that and the second JF opened his mouth, he shoved the whole bar in as far as he could.

At this stage Ginger recalled that he'd taken a hand in the proceedings.

It was all pretty nasty and more than a bit frightening at the time, but looking back now he was quite proud of the part he had played. Although it didn't seem such a big thing at the time, he'd managed to hold his own against Leverett that night

He was standing next to JF and as Leverett turned away to hand back the unused part of the soap, Ginger grabbed the bit from JF and stuffed it under the blankets of the nearest bed.

JF played his part too and when he got Leveretts attention again, he went through the motions of chewing and pulling the most agonising faces, until at last Leverett told him to go and wash his mouth out in the bathroom. JF had the taste of the soap in his mouth even if he didn't have the actual soap to contend with. He didn't need a second invitation to get to the bathroom, he was away like a scalded cat.

'He didn't chew that soap sir. It's under those blankets sir.'

The hangers-on chorus were scoring points quicker than a dart player consistently hitting treble top.

Leverett stepped forward and lifted up the corner of the blankets, exposing the chunk of soap. It was right next to where Ginger was standing; he could see the teeth marks where JF had bitten it off.

'What's this then. How did that get here?' he demanded.

He was angry. His little joke had fallen flat; someone had put one over on him. He did the jokes. Someone was playing him at his own game.

He pushed his face right up close to Ginger's, his big snarling white teeth a stark contrast against his bright red face.

'It's a bit that fell off,' he told him, trying to sound innocent.

He recalled that at this stage he was scared witless but he had to try and bluff his way out of it. After all Leverett hadn't seen him put it there.

'It's not the bit he was chewing sir. It's a bit that fell off.' He said, trying to sound convincing.

'No it's not sir. It's the bit you told Yorkie to chew sir. He hid it under the blankets,' they chorused pointing at Ginger.

Quite what the hangers-on hoped to gain siding with him was a mystery. Leverett didn't have favourites, he growled at everyone.

'So you put it there did you?' he rasped. He was really angry by this time. The gee-up brigade had done their work well.

Now, with the benefit of hindsight, Ginger reflected that Leverett's hangers-on had always got away with telling tales on their messmates. They had never been beaten up or anything, they had just been accepted. Everyone knew who they were. It was no secret. There was always two and sometimes three of them.

The ring leader was Gillette. He was short, fat and ugly. His pig like face sweated all the time. His body seemed too long in proportion to his little short legs. When he walked he leaned forward. Behind his back they called him 'Duck's Arse'.

The first time Leverett had come in on an old motor bike, he had asked for volunteers to clean it for him and it was 'Duck's Arse' who had jumped straight up and volunteered himself and his two side-kicks. That old bike was filthy and the trio of grovellers came back to the mess hours later, covered in grease and muck, with not a thing gained from an entire Sunday afternoon spent in Leverett's employ.

Ginger could see them all quite clearly in his minds eye as he sat on his bed thinking back. Particularly the faces. JF's face as he got the taste of that soap; Gillette's face as he almost fell over his own feet in his eagerness to tell on his mates. But above all Leveretts snarling teeth only inches away from his face.

'So you decided to hide the soap under the blankets did you,' Leverett snarled again.

He felt that he was very small and vulnerable at that stage. It was never a good idea to get ones self into the limelight and particularly to get Leverett's full attention. He remembered vividly standing in front of Leverett, shame faced and being very close to tears. Leverett had that effect on people.

'I told you sir, it was just a bit that fell off. I picked it up in case someone slipped on it.'

He was lying. Everyone knew it but he had to try to put on a brave face. Leverett had no right to make them eat soap. Although he was terrified of Leverett when he was in one of those moods, something forced him to brazen it out. Leverett guessed that he had been lying but there was not much he could do about it. Even the hangers-on had gone quiet.

'Right then, as you're so public spirited—YOU chew the soap. There it is then. Get on with it.'

Once more Leverett looked round with that false smile of his, willing others to laugh with him. Once more he was met with a stony silence.

'No.' said Ginger

It was rather too loud to sound convincing. The chunk of soap still lay where it was.

Leverett turned abruptly on his heels to face him.

'No. You dare to say no to me. Chew on that soap before I force it right down your throat.'

By this stage Ginger remembered he was almost choking with fear, but he managed to put on a brave front. He knew he was in pretty deep by this time and there was no telling what Leverett might do next.

'No. I won't eat soap. I've done nothing wrong,' he replied defiantly.

'We'll see about that lad. You bite that soap right now or you'll be on a charge.'

It was as if Leverett had run out of ideas.

Ganges boys were like sheep and normally did whatever they were told to do without hesitation. Ginger's defiance had thrown him off course.

Ginger had even surprised himself. He didn't ever remember being that brave before but he had let himself get in too deep until there was no way out. He recalled that his only course of action was to carry on.

'I've done nothing wrong sir. If you put me on a charge I shall tell the DO that you made me chew soap for no reason,' he countered.

He didn't really think that one would work. The DO would back up Leverett anyway and undoubtedly Batchelor would have to involve himself. He felt very lonely; he wished he hadn't got involved. He was just trying to help his pal. Meanwhile JF had wisely stayed in the bathroom out of the way.

Suddenly, quite out of the blue, Leverett changed the subject.

'Right then, time to turn in. Get those beds made up. Lights out in five minutes', he said, brushing boys aside as he strode away along the length of the mess.

Ginger was shaking all over but he tried not to show it. He guessed that this was only an interlude and that pretty soon Leverett would be back at him again.

But nothing happened.

Leverett marched to the bottom of the mess and back again without saying a word. They didn't realise it then but he was beaten. He had overstepped his authority and he knew it. A minute or so later he turned out the lights and without the usual 'goodnight', he departed in silence. The incident was never mentioned again.

Sitting on his bed and recalling that incident once again, Ginger felt some satisfaction. With the benefit of hindsight and with a bit of 'service' under his belt, he felt good. Despite not feeling very brave at the time, he had managed to stick one right up Leverett.

That nasty bastard deserved all he got.

Chapter 13

Ganges boys could dance the hornpipe possibly better than anyone else on earth and, to its credit, it had to be said that the sight of a large squad of young lads all kitted out exactly the same and all dancing a set routine to music, with arm and leg movements coordinated as one man was a spectacle seldom equalled.

But there was no pleasure for the boys in this dance spectacular that was witnessed by hundreds, if not thousands, of 'civvies' at regattas, garden parties or any other function where a free display could be cajoled from one of the wardroom's many chinless wonders.

That merry little dance so beloved of people who didn't have to perform in it, had been perfected over weeks and weeks of intensive training and torture in the gym. Torture in two senses of the word.

The physical kind where aching leg muscles were forced to go on and on, even after what seemed much longer than the hour that they had been pumping up and down and also the mental torture that comes from knowing one false step or momentary stumble would result in the whole squad having at least another twenty minutes added on '.... to go through the whole routine once again.'

Yes, Ganges boys could dance the hornpipe perfectly in public but if only people had known what went on in the privacy of the gym and what price the boys had to pay to bring the onlookers that kind of precision.

Maze marching was another particular favourite that always went down well. This was yet another stupid dance routine. Maze marching was performed at breakneck speed and with even more complicated and intricate manoeuvres than that rotten hornpipe.

Vast numbers of boys were drilled and drilled in a complex routine of marching, counter marching and forming complicated patterns within their ranks until they could do it like trained monkeys, neither knowing or caring what they were doing or why. They were just happy in the knowledge that when it was right everyone was happy and that made life fractionally better all round.

Occasionally after a particularly productive session they would get a 'well done' from the PT officer and that was good news. Not that any of them cared if they had done well or not. It wasn't praise they were looking for but once those cherished words had been uttered there was nothing anyone else could say to the contrary.

Generally the PT staff were not too bad. Sure, they were instructors but they only took PT classes and the rest of the time they didn't bother the boys. They had their own business to attend to in the gym so with them it was 'out of sight—out of mind'.

49 mess had done their share of gymnasium work. They'd progressed through the basic syllabus and had moved on to the more complex routines where, as far as they were concerned, they had more than held their own.

It was just a matter of keeping fit really. Not that they needed special procedures for keeping fit considering they were obliged to double march everywhere, all day every day. That amount of running about was enough to keep anyone fit—and just in case it wasn't, there was organised sports every afternoon.

What with all the sport and the incidental doubling everywhere, the boys considered they were fit enough but the Navy had other ideas and that was where the PTIs played their part.

Gymnasium work was part of the training programme and had to be undertaken. It held its own special place on the curriculum but it was easy enough compared to many other parts of their training programme. Easy in that they were fit enough to go through the sessions almost as if by remote control and in some respects they could relax, relatively speaking, in the gym because there wasn't Leverett or Batchelor looking over their shoulder.

Maybe it was that complacency that was their downfall. Maybe it was because they knew Leverett wouldn't be behind them or maybe they figured that the PTIs would be more lenient toward them. Who could tell, but whatever the reasons they remained unspoken.

There didn't appear to be any reason to put their thoughts into words. It was as if some sixth sense had enveloped them and they all knew exactly what they were going to do—or rather, on this occasion, what they were not going to do.

They were going to give the next session a miss and skive off down on the foreshore. Although it was a bit nippy, it was still quite a pleasant day and sod the gym anyway; they probably wouldn't be missed. They'd done so much gym work they knew it backwards. They were good at it. The box, the parallel bars, the ropes and, naturally, those Maze Marching routines; they knew it all.

Even the Divisional PTI, who had acquired the name of 'Mighty Mouse' due to his size, or rather the lack of it, had said they were good. It was nothing to boast about.

It didn't impress any of them but it did mean that they had outpaced their

119

instructor and they were up to the required standard well ahead of time.

That in turn meant, to their minds at least, that there was no point in turning up any more and so that was the course of action they decided upon.

They should have known better.

They were missed.

Of course they were missed. Anything out of the ordinary was bound to be spotted immediately. They were all well acquainted with routines and most of them adapted quite naturally but on this occasion they had made a serious miscalculation of judgement—both theirs and their instructors.

Ganges was run on routine. There were routines for everything. The entire regime was very regimented and everything in the place worked to a routine. Even what seemed like routine for the sake of routine was tolerated. Routine became an everyday way of life. But one routine they didn't expect and certainly didn't want, was the dreaded Shotley Routine.

They had sailed a bit close to the wind a few times in the past and that had incurred the wrath of Leverett. That was bad enough but Shotley Routine was something else.

Talk about jumping out of the frying pan and into the fire, that was exactly what they had done. Then, just to make matters worse, on that occasion the frying pan was hardly warm.

All they had to do was to make their way round to No. 1 gym and go through an easy session with their PTI. 'Mighty Mouse' had run out of ideas anyway; he didn't want them there any more than they wanted to be there. But instead of just going along, they were taking things into their own hands and heading for deep trouble.

There had been murmurings of discontent about doing PT classes but why it should have come to a head at that particular juncture, was anyone's guess. Maybe having been left to make their own way round to the gym had some bearing on it. During their first few weeks Jury or Leverett would have marched them everywhere but class leaders had been appointed and they were expected to turn up at various activities unsupervised.

Daisy was the one to turn thoughts into words.

'I can't see any point going down to the gym,' he said.

It was during mid morning stand-easy. There wasn't much time left to change into PT gear and so far none of them had made the effort.

'We shall have to get that heavy box out and run round in circles, jumping over it, just like we did last time we were in there,' he continued. ' No-one is very interested in us anyway; even 'Mighty Mouse' don't know what to do with us.'

'Just take last time we were there,' chipped in Mac.

Mac, the blond Londoner had the most uncoordinated body Ginger had ever seen. His antics made Mick Southern look positively smooth. Mac's thin arms and legs seemed to have a mind of their own. A gymnast is the last thing that would spring to mind when describing his talents. But they had gone over the same old stuff so many times that eventually Mac got it right and if Mac had got it right then the remainder of them certainly had.

'That's right,' interrupted JF. 'Old 'Mighty Mouse' even buggered off and left us on our own because he didn't know what else to get us to do.'

'We'll give it a miss then,' said Daisy.

Daisy was only a small lad but he had emerged as a front runner. PO Jury had made him their leading boy.

Daisy was once again in front and leading the way, as had become his style. Now he was planning to lead them in the wrong direction; the course of action he had in mind could cost him his badge.

Not one of the renegades realised just how serious the situation was. To turn up late for a class without a very good reason was almost a hanging offence, but to skip a session altogether—well!

It was doubtful if such a thing had happened before in the entire history of the place.

That was the plan. They would skive off and keep right out of the way until midday and everyone would be pleased because they would get a free period and not have to worry about them.

But a complete class not being where they were supposed to be and furthermore no sign of them anywhere else either was bound to attract attention. Although they were not to know, their disruption of routine activated major panic stations.

That was the plan but unfortunate for them the Navy does not think along those lines and they were missed within the first few minutes and a full scale search organised to locate them.

There was just a chance they had gone to the wrong classes. Perhaps they'd succumbed to some mystery illness in the mess .... maybe there had been an accident .... surely an entire class hadn't gone on the trot.

The first they were aware of how popular they had become was when the Tannoy broadcast 'Hands to Dinner.'

They'd had enough sense to wait until the very last minute before returning to the mess and to cut down on their chances of detection, they had managed to work their way along so that when they broke cover it would look as if they were coming from the direction of the gym.

It was all good stuff and well thought out. But all to no avail.

They made their way from behind the gymnasia block and across the road toward the outside heads between Hawke and Collingwood then, within sight of safety—they ran slap bang into PO Jury.

'Where the hell have you been?'

Cyril Jury could shout when the occasion demanded and apparently, this was such an occasion. He rarely showed any emotion, but right now seemed to be the exception. His face betrayed his feelings.

Jury was really upset; this was not the reception they had expected. They didn't expect to receive public thanks for giving them all a couple of hours rest with nothing to do, but at the same time they didn't expect to get screamed at. They hadn't stopped to think it right through and naturally they expected to be told off a bit when other people were listening. But that softening of his face, that tight little smile of his, the merest inclination of his head in a nod of approval, would have told them all they wanted to know. But this was something else. Jury was livid.

There was no-one else about. They were sheltered by Hawke block on one side and the toilet wall on the other side. No-one could see or hear them but still he tore into them; he was absolutely furious. Whatever was wrong with the man.

'Well,' he demanded. 'Where the hell have you been? Do you realise you've had half the people in the place out looking for you?'

Jury always stood to attention in front of them when he was being 'official', it was his way. But this time his personal feelings far outweighed his normal Navy-through-and-through front. He didn't appear to be able to stand still for any length of time. Up and down he strode between the two walls; his face was bright red.

He was taking this whole thing very hard. He was visibly upset; he looked close to tears. But why?

If it had been Leverett or Batchelor that had found them, they would have expected this kind of attitude. After all those two did it as a matter of course. The boys would have stood there letting the waves of venom sweep over them until the little episode played itself out.

But PO Jury was different. He normally showed very little emotion but he was taking their little escapade very personally and they couldn't reason out why.

They still couldn't see what all the fuss was about; they hadn't done anything so bad. Jury was genuinely upset, there was no doubt about that but it appeared to be more from frustration and disappointment than anger. They couldn't understand it. They felt no remorse about their actions, it still didn't seem such a big deal.

The fact that they would be found out sooner or later was in the back of their mind when they embarked upon their excursion of free initiative, but actually getting caught still came as a bit of a shock.

But so what. They'd been caught before.

Like the time they were caught playing sledges with tubular steel chairs on the polished deck, when they were housed in that temporary mess in Benbow Lane. That time they had got away lightly. Apart from a few laps of the parade ground, at the double and in their own time, plus a trip over the mast, all they had to do was spend a few days buffing all the scratches out of that polished surface and making it look like new again.

But that was in the past. They were old hands now and brazen enough not to care what Ganges could throw at them.

What was worrying was Cyril Jury. Why was he so upset? Seeing him like that was beginning to get to them; they had never planned to do anything to displease him. If it was Leverett that would have been different. They didn't give a toss about his feelings anyway. Cyril they liked, as far as they could ever like an instructor and they were more concerned about having upset him than they were about the prospect of 'Jankers' that now seemed inevitable.

PO Jury was finding it difficult to speak. A couple of times he turned his face away mid-sentence, almost as if he couldn't bear to continue.

Suddenly he cleared his throat.

'Well, if you've got nothing to say for yourselves, you had best be getting over to the CMG for dinner, before it's too late. After dinner you will remain in the mess until I decide what to do with you.'

Jury didn't want to talk and none of the boys felt brave enough to speak to him. He told them to go and that was exactly what they did. They didn't need a second invitation to get away.

In the CMG the midday meal was eaten in silence, there was none of the usual chatter that accompanied every other meal they had ever eaten in the place. PO Jury's words were still ringing in their ears. Finally the penny had dropped and the seriousness of the situation was becoming more apparent by the minute.

For the first time since they had arrived in Hawke Division their appetites failed them. The Navy was never over generous with the feeding of the boys and each meal was designed to be just enough to carry them along until the next one was due. This time Ginger was just going through the motions and he guessed that the others were doing the same.

The dinner was eaten mechanically almost as if by remote control with none of them remembering what it was they were eating. The pudding suffered the same fate as the dinner. They hardly even looked at the food that was placed before them; the eyes saw but the brain didn't register. They had more important things on their minds.

A large class of boys but with one single train of thought:

What had they done that was so bad and what was to be their fate? They made their way back to 49 mess after dinner was finished and they did so in complete silence. As they walked along the back of Nelson Hall, despite their numbers, each of them was alone and completely engrossed in his own thoughts.

As one mind, they were speculating on what lie ahead.

Back in the mess there was little evidence of their earlier bravado and when someone suggested changing into sports rig before PO Jury came back, there was no opposition to the idea. Suddenly none of them were prepared to rock the boat any further.

Once again it was Daisy who put thoughts into words.

'We'd better make sure we're all changed and have clean gear on before he comes back. We don't want any more trouble than we've already got. Let's not give him an excuse to pile anything else on to us.'

'Yeh,' agreed Dereham, 'we don't want to upset him any more than he is already do we.'

He often put a statement in the form of a question.

Dereham liked the high profile approach and to be in the centre of things. He liked to run with the ring leaders, whatever their point of view might be. He would even transfer his allegiance mid-argument if the opposition looked like coming out on top. He wasn't the brightest of people but he had bulk to back up his views.

Dereham was a bully, or at least he would have been if he had enough brain power to put forward a convincing argument. But this time he was right, they didn't want to antagonise Jury any further.

'Maybe he'll have calmed down a bit now that he has had his dinner,' said Gillette realising that he would be in trouble too.

His fat face was sweating profusely; his grovelling status was in jeopardy.

'Just in case why don't we tidy up the mess a bit. He always notices things like that.'

'Yeh,' echoed Dereham, 'let's square up the mess a bit so it looks good when he comes in. He always notices things like that. Someone check the bathroom and airing room while the rest of us square off the beds and bedding.'

It was unnecessary for Dereham to have said anything. Gillette had just said all that. Dereham was throwing his weight around again. It was easy to give orders when the idea had already been floated and all had given their approval.

When someone supplied the ammunition Dereham loved to fire the gun, it got him noticed and made him feel important. He talked loud and loved to give orders—after the decisions had been made by someone else of course. He was usually the one to fire the gun providing someone supplied him with ammunition first. He didn't possess the brain power to manufacture his own.

At one of their compulsory church services, the 'Sin Bosun' had been labouring the point '.... and some fell upon stony ground' and ever since, whenever Ginger heard that phrase it always reminded him of Dereham. With Dereham it was all stony ground.

'He told us to stay in the mess after dinner,' said Daisy, 'I wonder if we should fall-in down below when the bugle goes or if he meant that we should stay here until someone tells us different.'

Mick Southern usually had something to add to proceedings but Mick's face looked as blank as his mind appeared to be on the subject. It seemed that they were all waiting for someone else to make a decision.

As usual Dereham had no opinion and he wouldn't have until the whole thing had been finalised. PO Jury put an end to the speculation.

Just as the Tannoy buzzed into life, he appeared at the head of the stairs. His anger had subsided and the redness had left his face but his eyes were cold and staring; his lips taut and unsmiling.

'Come on then, whatcha waiting for. Down below, quick as you can. Come on. Move, move, move.'

He usually looked around the mess. This time he didn't. He didn't step inside the door. All their extra effort spent in tidying up had been in vain, he hadn't noticed. Their little bit of attempted grovelling had failed miserably. He didn't even notice their clean sports gear.

The boys clattered down the stairs and fell in outside the door, in their usual place. Not a word was spoken but each of them was conscious of doing everything exactly right. For a change—and probably for the first time ever—they were the first mess fallen in correctly and standing perfectly still, properly at ease, tallest on the flanks and shortest in the centre.

Point scoring time was over though. Jury walked down the stairs and straight past them without even raising his eyes. Leverett was already in the colonnade and was busy talking to other instructors further along. Jury joined him.

Batchelor appeared round the corner from the Divisional Office and the instructors went into the usual routine of calling their mess to attention and reporting to him, before moving away to their various sporting activities.

Soon they were the only ones left in the colonnade.

The situation reminded Ginger of their first day in Hawke. That day everything was new to them and now it felt like that first afternoon all over again.

PO Jury hadn't called them to attention or reported to Batchelor. He and Leverett had moved closer to them when the activity started and now that they were alone, Batchelor joined them.

'Right then,' began Jury.

It was the first time he had spoken since leaving the mess.

'Wait Petty Officer,' interrupted Batchelor.

His trade mark, the scowl, was fully visible as he strode up and down in front of them.

Those three words were enough. Every single boy assembled knew in that instant that they were in trouble. Batchelor was on top of things; his scowl gave the game away. He was on one of his ego trips. He had a whole squad of boys that everyone knew were guilty. He could scream and shout at them as much as he liked without having to worry who might overhear him. He had a squad of boys to be punished and he was in his element, already loving every minute of it.

'Well you've really done it this time. I knew this class was heading for serious trouble .... now you've landed yourselves in it. I've had my eye on you for some time. You just won't learn will you I always knew you were the trouble makers .... Yak, yak, yak; yeh, yeh, yeh; blah, blah, blah.'

That kraut voice was really giving the treatment; that nasal growl blasting down his nose was in full swing. They stood there because they had to, not caring and most of them not even listening.

They knew they were in a lot of trouble as soon as he poked himself in but his shouting added nothing extra. Batchelor was evil where boys who couldn't answer back were concerned, but the boys of 49 mess had learned to let him shout himself out without getting upset about it any more.

They were in trouble, deep trouble. They all knew it. They also knew that Batchelor would make their time under punishment as memorable for them as possible. But they also knew that all the time he was standing still belching venom at them they were not doing anything else. They still had to do exactly as he told them but now it was just inconvenient, they were not afraid of him any longer.

'Well, what do you think you were playing at?' he growled.

No-one moved. No-one said a word. Most of them had probably switched off. They were old hands now. Let him get stuffed.

'Well, the DO has something in mind for you, but for the moment, up to the mess and put your boots on and get back down here as quickly as you can. Right then, carry on Petty Officer.'

Jury called the boys to attention and saluted Batchelor.

'Right then, you heard the officer. Up to the mess and get your boots on. Away you go then, move, move, move.'

They knew what that meant. There would be no sports for them that afternoon. They were only expected to wear their boots in the afternoon when they were Duty Division work party. They were not Duty Division, so that only left one other possibility and Batchelor's continued presence only confirmed what they already knew.

When they fell in again wearing their boots, Jury and Leverett had gone. Batchelor had them all to himself.

'Right then. Fall in and stand still.'

As soon as he was faced by three ranks of boys all standing perfectly still, that Kraut Voice snarled out again as he called them to attention.

'Left turn. Quick march.'

They turned left and headed out from under the colonnade toward the swimming bath. His next order had them wheeling left and heading on to the parade ground, parallel to the POs' mess.

The next order 'Double March,' confirmed, if there was ever any doubt, what they guessed from the start.

Although at that stage it was still unofficial, they were on Shotley Routine— and their first session was already underway.

Chapter 14

Shotley Routine was a right cow.

The boys of 49 mess had always had it a bit harder than most of the other messes and they'd come to accept that as a matter of course. This unfortunate state of affairs was due to Leverett's continual presence and Batchelor's sixth sense of always being in the right place at the right time or, depending from whose eyes the situation was viewed, the wrong place at the wrong time.

They had learned how to ride the rough spots of the normal everyday routine without letting the situation get to them and even their first 'unofficial' session on Shotley Routine they had taken in their stride. Although it was all new to them, what was there that could be different from what they had done a hundred times before when Batchelor or Leverett had been in one of their sadistic moods.

No-one had actually said Shotley Routine. They all knew they were about to get a dose of it; the phrase had been bandied about continually ever since their non-appearance at the gym.

They knew they were lumbered but there was no actual moment when it became official. They just kind of drifted quietly into it.

As quietly as it ever got with Kraut Voice and Gob 'n' Gaiters around anyway.

Batchelor had taken great delight in introducing them to their first session. He had the knack of making everything worse than it needed to be and that time he had employed all his horrible, underhanded ways to make things as difficult as possible.

He really did take great delight in causing people anguish. He was quite possibly a torture chamber attendant in a previous life.

Possibly their actual punishment routine hadn't meant to be started until the following morning but Batchelor didn't care. He'd had a squad of boys all to himself all afternoon. He was in his glory and he could give full vent to his hatred of boys.

There was nothing new to being drilled by Batchelor anyway. They had all been there before—usually when they had done nothing wrong, so knowing that they were in the wrong and had been well and truly caught, made him a little easier to bear.

Sessions with Batchelor were not that much of a problem anyway not now they had become accustomed to him and his sadistic ways. They were inconvenient and there were far better ways of spending a couple of hours than helping him to act out his petty fantasies. They were inconvenient but not difficult.

They all knew that he wouldn't allow them to double march around him all afternoon, there was no fun for him in that. He wanted boys to be strictly under his control and to achieve that state he had to continually give orders, he wasn't aware of it but that was his only mistake as far as the boys were concerned. Continual drill and carrying out various parade ground manoeuvres was far easier than the monotonous doubling round and round in silence.

Pretty soon they had cottoned on how to let his venom sweep over them without allowing any of it to sink in and affect them. His nastiness and non-stop hatred was mainly for his own benefit anyway. Most of it they didn't even hear any more.

The fact that they could all do that parade drill in their sleep made the time pass quickly and fairly easily.

But if they thought time on Shotley Routine was all going to be that easy, they had a shock waiting for them.

Yes, Shotley Routine was a right cow.

They got their first taste of what they had let themselves in for, early the next morning. Very early

Leverett woke them up; he was in a foul mood. As usual when he was duty instructor he was shaved, his boots were polished and his suit pressed. He was ready for the day ahead.

The lights burst into life and the dustbin went crashing down the centre of the mess, propelled by a highly polished boot.

'Well come on then, let's be having yer outa those stinking pits. It's not a bloody holiday camp; you're not on yer daddies yacht now. In this mans Navy you jump when I say jump. Come on then, out, out, out.'

He strode purposefully all the way down to the bottom of the mess and back up again, kicking the dustbin in front of him as he went. But they were old hands now. They had been in for nearly three months and that kind of performance didn't impress them any more.

A few sat up in bed but the majority didn't even move. They knew that the duty instructor just came in and woke them up and then left straight away to do likewise in the other messes of the Division. They also knew they were safe in bed for another ten minutes or so.

But this time it was Leverett and he didn't leave. He was angry about something and the fact that no-one took any notice of him made his temper even worse.

'Well come on then, I'm not talking for my own benefit. Out, come on out,

out, everybody out. Last one out goes over the mast.'

That last bit got their attention. No-one wanted an early morning trip up the mast in their pyjamas.

'Where d'ya think you're going,' he screamed at a few boys who were heading for the bathroom. 'Stand still. Everybody stand at the foot of your beds, stop cackling your fat and stand still.'

When they were all standing at the foot of their respective beds, he walked slowly past them; his hobnailed boots sounding very loud in the stillness of the early morning.

'Right then, towel round yer neck and fall in down below in the colonnade.'

For a few seconds no-one moved. Fall in down below. Whatever for? He must be having some kind of joke with them.

'Well come on then, unless you'd all like to go over the mast first.'

He wasn't joking. He was bright red with anger, the veins on his neck looked ready to burst.

They scrambled downstairs and fell in, shivering outside in the colonnade. The eerie stillness of the morning was something new to them, there was not a sound of life anywhere. Then, as if by Devine inspiration, the situation became clear to them. He had got them up early before 'wakey wakey' had been broadcast over the Tannoy.

That was what was different; they hadn't heard 'Charlie' being played over the loudspeakers. That was why there was no-one else about; everyone else was still asleep.

After a minute or so, Leverett followed them down. He was still in that agitated state.

'It's a cold shower for you lot in the swimming bath.'

Someone in the rear rank gave a long sorrowful moan at the thought.

Leveretts face and neck turned purple with rage.

'Who said that? Come on, which of you did that?' he bellowed.

No-one moved; no-one spoke. He walked up the assembled ranks staring at each boy in turn, looking for a tell-tale sign; there was none. His glare was met by three rows of blank innocent faces.

'Well, whoever it was, you've only got yourselves to blame. You've been warned enough times and now you've got what you deserve. You're on Shotley Routine. You brought it on yourselves and now you've got to pay.'

That's what it was all about. Ginger had forgotten all about Shotley Routine. It had gone completely out of his mind overnight.

They guessed they were heading for it but nothing had actually been said and even that episode with Batchelor was behind them. Overnight he had forgotten all about it. He expected they would have to go before the Commander or someone first, but as nothing further had been said he figured that it would probably take a few days before coming official.

He hadn't bargained for this. He didn't know that it would start at this hour of the morning. Now it was all beginning to make sense to him, the reason for Leverett's bad mood and everything. It didn't take much to get him into a bad mood. This would be enough to raise his temper; if they had to get up early, so did he.

None of them knew what Shotley Routine was like. They'd heard the rumours but now it was serious business and not a joking matter any more.

Their little escapade of skipping gym classes had been the final straw in getting them a dose of the famous Shotley Routine but unwittingly they had lumbered their instructors with it too.

All the getting up early, the work and extra drills they had as part of the punishment, the instructors had to be there as well. That certainly was not good news.

It was only just beginning to sink in what they had let themselves in for but Leverett knew. He knew that they had let him in for it as well.

It was all new to them, they didn't know. Leverett knew and he was not the type to forget, but more to the point he would make sure they didn't forget either.

Leverett allowed a long pause to let his words sink in. Although it was June, the morning air was very cold and that cold was also sinking in. It seemed quite a while before he ordered shivering boys to turn left and head off into the swimming bath door.

There was no heating in the changing room that early in the day but it was a lot better than standing outside on the concrete of the colonnade in bare feet, with nothing more substantial than pyjamas to keep out the cold.

Ginger made use of the temporary respite to sit on the wooden slats that served as seats and rub some life back into his cold feet. But the respite was short lived and as soon as the last of them was in Leveretts voice rang out again.

'Right then, off pyjamas and into the showers.'

The showers were in one big room, leading off the changing room. It had tiled floor and walls and shower heads high up near the ceiling. There were no individual cubicles. The water was regulated by a valve near the door, on the changing room side. Leverett turned it to the 'cold' position and stood alongside, with his hand on the handle.

They filed into the freezing cold downpour; there was no way to avoid getting wet because the showers all worked together and sprayed the entire area.

Usually it was quite pleasant going through the showers after a swim, but this time it was different. The water was cold and so was the atmosphere. They shuffled slowly toward the far wall and then back again toward the door and a dry towel. But at the door Leverett barred the way.

'I'll tell you when,' he sneered.

They had forced him to get up early and now they were going to pay.

The cold had penetrated while they were standing outside in the colonnade and now, standing in freezing water with more continually pouring over them they were really cold and beginning to feel ill. But still they were obliged to suffer until his sadism was satisfied.

After what seemed like an eternity and all movement from the boys had ceased, the water stopped. Leverett turned the valve off.

'Right then. Out the door one at a time with your hand above your head.'

He was deliberately doing anything he could to prolong the agony.

In the changing room he made them all stand naked until the last one was out of the shower room and had gone through his pretence of being inspected. Then, striding to the outside door he threw it wide open with a crash.

'Right then, everyone back up to the mess and get dressed as quickly as possible.'

They were almost numb with cold and couldn't get away quick enough. Most of them just grabbed up their pyjamas and towel and made a dash for the mess and the welcoming warmth of the airing room that lay just across the road.

Yes, Shotley Routine really was a right cow and now they had first hand experience.

They were all dressed and sitting on their beds when the first strains of 'Charlie' burst forth from the Tannoy accompanied by the sounds and shouts associated with the first noises of the day filling the morning air.

'Charlie' was a bit late for the inhabitants of 49 mess they were already wide awake courtesy of Petty Officer Leverett and the cold shower.

They had survived their first real session of the new punishment routine. Now they had thawed out and they were ready to let the rest of the Division know who the new tough guys around the place were.

Ten minutes earlier it would have been a different story, but no-one had seen them then.

The days that followed were filled with continual activity, with what seemed like never a moment to spare.

If they ever thought that the early rising and cold shower was the low point of the day, they were sadly disillusioned. Now that they were on Shotley

Routine their days started badly and then got steadily worse. Everyone knew they were on Shotley Routine and they were never allowed to forget that fact; from the time they got up until they went to bed at night they were continuously on the move.

At least once they were in bed they were there for the night.

A few years earlier, they had been told, they would have been woken up every two hours for a half hour trip round the parade ground. Thankfully that little gem had been discontinued—probably because it meant that the instructor had to get up as well.

Their bed was like a sanctuary; a time capsule that took them away from everything for a few hours. Now that they were under punishment there was none of the usual skylarking and talking in the evenings. As soon as their last muster of the day was over they fell into bed as if pole-axed, where they lay until the following morning when it would start all over again.

Shotley Routine meant there was no free time to themselves at all; no sports in the afternoon and no picture show in No.1 gymnasium.

Despite not being allowed to go and watch their favourite Tom and Jerry cartoons, the gymnasium played a big part. Whenever the instructor couldn't find anything to do with them, they would find themselves down in the gym. There was always spare PTIs wandering about and usually they were glad of something to do.

Knowing that 49 mess was there as part of their punishment, they made the sessions a bit more difficult with emphasis on the strength sapping manoeuvres.

The boys knew that they would spend long periods hanging with their backs to the wall bars and their legs extended out at right angles to their body or suspended from ropes attached to roof beams until aching muscles could take no more. Another favourite was to make them pass a heavy wooden bench over their heads, side to side, until they couldn't keep it up any longer.

It was poetic justice in a way. They were suddenly spending far more time in the gym than ever before and the reason they were on Shotley Routine was for skipping gym in the first place.

Each instructor had his own ideas about how boys on Shotley Routine should be treated. Leverett was the worst of the Hawke Division by a short head from Batchelor. They were both evil and sadistic but Leverett got the vote because he liked people to suffer.

Batchelor also wanted the boys to suffer but he blotted his copybook by wanting to get involved. He was not content to just let them double up and down; he wanted to control them every second and that was his big mistake. He had to have power. He would have them stand still at attention or at ease, for long periods until he was satisfied that they were doing it correctly. Or he would have them practice saluting, taking ages to adjust each individuals fingers and arm angle. He was even idiot enough to stand in front of them demonstrating how he wanted certain manoeuvres carried out. His venom and hatred of boys would be belching forth all the time, but at least they were standing still for long periods.

By contrast Leverett just wanted suffering. He was content to stand still and let them double around him until someone dropped.

On the Saturday night after supper it was pouring with rain when Leverett came up to the mess for them. The rain prevented them from going on the parade ground and they had laid their kit out for inspection earlier in the day so they knew there would be no point in him making them lay it out again so soon after. Therefore the odds looked in favour of going to the gym again. They knew there was pictures in No.1 gym on Saturdays, so the small No.3 gym looked to be the most obvious solution.

They were wearing a full blue serge suit and the next move looked to be a change into sports rig. But that was not the case. Leverett already had a plan, he must have thought of it as he was walking over from the POs' mess. He was wearing his oilskin coat as he came in and soon they would be wearing theirs too.

'On oilskins, sling respirators, carry tin hats and fall in down below.'

They had not had to touch their respirators before except once when they tested them, soon after they were issued. Ginger figured that must be what he had planned for them again. Just something to do as it was raining hard. It looked to him as if they might be going to the gas bunker again.

It would still not be a bed of roses though, Leverett would make sure of that. He was sure to make them stay in the bunker longer than was necessary when he released the gas canister. He would make them remove their respirators and stand in the gas until they couldn't breathe, like he had last time but in any case it would soon be over and it would be a lot easier than racing round and round the parade ground.

Unfortunately that speculation was well off and their respirators were put to a slightly less orthodox use that night.

Leverett ordered them to button their oilskins right up to the neck and put their gas masks on and tin hat on their head. Then having marched over to Nelson Hall, the drill hall alongside the parade ground, he made them double march round and round inside until three of their numbers collapsed from exhaustion.

That was Leveretts style.

Fancy thinking they were going to get away lightly by just being half choked to death in the gas bunker.

Even to fit young lads who had been trained in suffering under Batchelor and Leverett, Shotley Routine was no picnic. Apart from their everyday routine of classes and time spent eating their meals, almost every waking moment was occupied in some way or another. They were not left alone at all until it was time for 'lights out' and they were allowed to climb, or rather drop, into their beds.

The physical suffering took preference and there was plenty of that but there was also the added joy of mental anguish to contend with. Mental suffering played almost as an important as the physical side of their punishment and Shotley instructors were experts in psychological terror.

Shotley Routine was the equivalent of Duty Division, Work Ship and a punishment routine all rolled into one—and then some.

It was hard. It was meant to be hard. It was designed to be hard and there was Leverett and Batchelor to ensure that it was hard.

There was no afternoon sports; there was no evening pictures and there was no Saturday or Sunday afternoon free time. Time to themselves was not on the Shotley Routine agenda.

There didn't appear to be any set down procedures to follow apart from the basic framework guidelines. Each instructor seemed to have his own version of the rules and his own idea of how they should be interpreted.

Sometimes a class from another division, apparently under a more lenient instructor, could be seen sweeping the Long Covered Way or picking up paper from the playing fields. There was even talk that an earlier class had been sent to the married quarters to tidy up gardens and cut lawns and the like, as part of their punishment under Shotley Routine.

Tales had circulated of times spent sitting out on the lawn tucking into cakes and lemonade. It was said that one class actually got to sweep and generally tidy up around the Captain's house with the Captain's wife serving the lemonade.

These tales only helped to make the boys of 49 mess even more unhappy. Who could tell. Maybe these stories were deliberately circulated as part of the psychological side of their punishment. In any case nothing like that ever happened to them while they were on the bugle.

Their less arduous periods—there were no easy periods where Leverett or Batchelor were concerned—were things like extra kit inspections and scrubbing the messdeck out from end to end. These would be forced on them during the periods that they would normally have been enjoying a picture show.

That kind of activity was always reserved for late at night which meant that the instructor could go away for an hour or so and then inspect the finished product any time they felt inclined to do so. They knew how long any given task would take and they always managed to turn up again on or before the prescribed time limit, thereby ensuring the boys didn't have enough time to complete the assignment and get a few minutes to relax as well.

On one such occasion, being left alone to scrub the wooden floorboards of the mess led the boys into a false sense of freedom. They still had the scrubbing to do but knowing they would be on their own for about an hour allowed them to relax a bit.

Normally they would scrub out in the Navy's time and have a full period to do it in. The mess wasn't dirty in any case; nothing in Ganges was ever dirty. There were two thousand boys to ensure that possibility never became a reality.

So, with that in the back of his mind and fairly safe in the knowledge that the duty instructor wouldn't be back for about an hour, Ginger had a brainwave.

The normal 'scrub-out' routine was to do one half of the mess at a time. Starting with the right hand side, all beds and lockers would be carried over and stood in between the beds on the other side.

That empty side would then be scrubbed and mopped until it was nearly dry. Then the procedure would be reversed and the left hand side transferred over and that side scrubbed.

But Ginger's wheeze called for a far simpler solution and it involved no humping about of beds.

'Lift all footwear up onto the beds and chuck a bucket of water down the mess,' he suggested. 'It'll only need about four buckets each side and then sweep it about until it dries in.'

Nobody had thought of that before and it was the perfect answer; ten minutes easy work instead of over an hour's hard slog. They went to it with a will, ensuring that there was no tell tale puddles or dry bits to give the game away.

The finished job looked perfect, just as good as if they had spent the full amount of time on it. They were crafty enough to leave the buckets and scrubbing brushes out near the door as if they had only just finished and they even remembered to take the wet broom away and hide it out of sight.

PO Jury was the duty instructor. As he climbed the stairs the word went out and they all busied themselves arranging the footwear back in straight lines under the beds. Another little ploy designed to make it look as if they had just finished.

As he entered through the door, Daisy, their badge boy, reported to him.

'Just finished sir. Mess scrubbed out like you ordered and we were just about to put the buckets and scrubbers away.'

Jury rarely showed any emotion, good or bad, he didn't smile much but on the other hand he didn't scowl like Batchelor or have his mouth turned down like Leverett. He had a 'neutral' face, one that was difficult to read anything from. It was almost as if he was afraid they might gain some advantage by being able to read what was on his mind from his facial expression.

He stopped just inside the door.

'Hummm,' he said more or less to himself, ignoring Daisy.

His gaze swept around the gathered faces; maybe they looked a little too cocksure or maybe Jury had a pessimistic nature.

Whatever the reason something triggered off suspicion in his mind.

He stepped a few paces forward and lifted the foot of the nearest bed off the floor, revealing two small round white circles where the legs had kept the floor dry. Their little ruse had been rumbled.

'Right then,' he said in that quiet way of his. 'Let's get those beds over to the other side and some hot soapy water on this deck. This time I'll wait.'

Their cleverness had gained them nothing but had cost them an extra hours work to do it all again. Apparently Jury had seen that old trick before.

Ginger was just glad that no-one remembered whose idea it was in the first place.

Chapter 15

Having anything more than five bob to spend in any week was quite a luxury, so going on leave with a whole pound for each week was like being in a different world. With three pound notes in their pocket and three weeks leave to spend it in, things were certainly looking rosy for the nozzers on leave morning.

It was the middle of August and their first leave. In fact it would be the first time they had been allowed outside the place in the three months since they joined.

All those romantic notions of Ginger's about going to town in his best suit were squashed by chief Bumble as soon as they were mentioned. Within their first couple of days they were left in no doubt along those lines. There was not even that game of darts or the leisurely drink in the canteen. They were going nowhere. They were soon put straight about that.

So home leave had taken on even more significance and had been a conversation piece for several weeks past but for the last few days the talk had been of little else.

Some of them had been too excited to sleep on their last night and had got dressed in their best suits ready to go, the minute the lights had been switched off.

Ginger had been as excited as any of them to get out of the place but nevertheless he had not been prepared to go without sleep all night. He hadn't wanted to be there almost from the moment he had arrived but he hadn't seen how going without sleep would help anything or make the morning come any quicker.

The morning came soon enough anyway.

Everyone in the mess was awake and sitting up in bed when the Tannoy buzzed into life.

On leave mornings they let a boy from the boys Bugle Band do the honours. Over the years it had become tradition that he was allowed, indeed even expected, to wake them up with 'Tiddley Charlie'—a jazzed-up version of Reveille. They were all ears. They'd heard about 'Tiddley Charlie' from some of the older hands and they were eager to experience it for themselves.

It was an experience all right. But whether the excitement came from hearing their first 'Tiddley Charlie' or because it heralded the start of leave, was hard to decide a few of the boys waved their arms about in time to the music, as if conducting the bugler from afar; a couple that were already out of bed were pretending to do a dance, a cross between a soft shoe shuffle and a tap dance. The vast majority of them were just sitting up in bed enjoying their first 'Tiddley Charlie', open mouthed.

Stirring and inspiring that it was, their leave morning musical awakening was all but forgotten half an hour later in their eagerness to get over to breakfast as early as possible. After breakfast anyone that was not already in their best suit changed as quickly as possible.

The Navy had worked out what train took who, where, who went in what direction and what time the train left. For those going through London they also told them what station and what time their connections were. There was nothing left to chance except, as usual, the boys were the only ones kept in the dark. They were classified into sections and only knew when they could leave when they were summoned to Nelson Hall ready for boarding a coach for the station.

Ginger's section—'The Norwich Group', only had about an hour to go on the train so they didn't get a packed lunch, known in naval circles as a 'bag-meal', but they still had to have their belongings searched.

They were told to take their No. 3 blue suit home and get it washed by mum, but apart from that and the small attaché case containing the Shotley Magazine and a couple of bars of nutty, they had nothing.

They were not allowed to keep personal belongings in Ganges; other than writing paper, envelopes and a pen, they had nothing. Batchelor and Leverett were always there to ensure they had nothing, but in Nelson Hall two crushers searched everyone's bag and case. They couldn't possibly find anything.

They filed past one table and were given a leave pass. A bit further along they were given six pound notes and a ten shilling note; the money was accompanied by a piece of paper stating that they were to hand over three pounds and ten shillings to their mum and to make sure they did mum had to sign the piece of paper to say that she had received the money.

Ginger's searcher was a big fat regulating petty officer and he made a thorough job of searching the dirty blue suit that was going home to be washed. After a while of grubbing about, he looked disappointed not to have found any contraband and grudgingly waved him through to board the coach.

The coach moved away immediately, through the Main Gate onto the road for Ipswich, the station and three weeks away from Batchelor, Leverett and Ganges.

He gave a sigh of relief. This was the life

Lowley and his ever present sidekick, 'Shiny' Black were in Ginger's compartment as the train pulled out of the station. As usual, Lowley had to be

139

centre of attention and it wasn't long before he was chasing up and down the corridor, doing his best to look like an old salt.

To help with his charade the first thing to get the treatment was his hat. The train had hardly started to move before his cap tally was removed and Ganges replaced with Defender. It was doubtful if Lowley knew where HMS Defender was, or in fact what it was. Where he had found that cap tally was a bit of a mystery, but at the same time, the thought of pretending he was off a ship never entered Ginger's head.

Lowley paraded up and down the corridor wearing his hat at a rakish angle at first and then flat-a-back, displaying the Defender tally, until he figured that everyone who was interested had seen him.

Then he returned to the compartment and produced a handful of assorted badges from his inside pocket. He selected one and after careful consideration, handed it to 'Shiny' Black. Puppy-dog Black must have already received instructions on the matter because he immediately got to work with needle and cotton to sew the badge on to Lowley's offered up sleeve.

Most of the 'Norwich Group' seemed to have the same idea and as they passed to and fro in the corridor, just popping their head in from time to time, Ginger was amazed to see they had all acquired instant promotion.

All manner of badges were on display, ranging from divers to air-crew. Some had even put them on the wrong arm. One fifteen year old had awarded himself a good conduct badge that no way could he have got until he was at least twenty-two.

Because he had no idea that the traffic in illegal badges went on, Ginger wondered if he had led a very sheltered life for the past three months. According to some of the older hands who had already been on leave before, it was traditional and happened every leave.

To the best of his knowledge none of the 49 mess boys knew anything about it. A few of them had acquired an odd cap tally that they had sewn on to their swimming trunks, but that was about the extent of their involvement.

If any of their lot were likely to be covered in badges it would be Dereham. Ginger had made a point of getting as far away from him as possible at the station, so he didn't know if Dereham had turned himself into a one man fleet or not.

After leave, on the return journey, the process was reversed and there was a mad scramble to remove all illegal decorations as quickly as possible, the moment the train was under way. They couldn't remove badges too soon as most of the boys had brought someone to see them off and they didn't want to lose face in the dying seconds of leave.

But as soon as the train wheels started to roll, scissors and razor blades went into action—they had to be quick, just in case any instructors were travelling back on the same train.

Ginger got roped in to help and wielding various razor blades helped to pass half an hour away. He had more important things on his mind; he was bringing back a pair of black plimsoles. The Navy issued white plimsoles, but his, wrapped up inside his newly washed and pressed blue suit, were civilian black ones

Three weeks had passed far too quickly and now, back off leave and into the familiar, if not entirely welcoming, confines of Hawke Division, he was keen to show of his new 'civvy' plimsoles. He'd spent seven shillings of his leave pay on them; they had come from the corner shop where until about six months previously he'd had a job delivering newspapers and groceries.

The plimsoles were a bit of a status symbol in a way. Not being Navy issue, they were not allowed and he knew it; everything they owned was Navy issue. That was what made them important to him, he had brought a little bit of home back with him. No-one else in the mess would have anything like it and he was in a hurry to get his boots off and his new informal footwear on.

It was about four o'clock and many of the boys were not back yet. The ones that were back were busy unpacking their gear and changing out of their best suits. He wasn't in a hurry to change apart from his boots. He quickly chucked them off and put his new plimsoles on.

He could see Daisy right down at the bottom end of the mess; he hoped he looked casual as he sauntered over.

'Had a good leave then, Daisy?'

He tried to be casual but the excitement of wearing his new plimsoles and waiting for someone to notice, made his voice a couple of octaves higher as he almost shouted the greeting.

There were several others nearby and he casually rested his foot on the end rail of the nearest bed, willing anyone to notice and mention his new plimsoles.

'Yeh, OK mate. I had a great time,' replied Daisy without looking up from what he was doing. 'What about you? You seem full of yourself.'

'First class,' Ginger said, at the same time allowing his foot to 'accidentally' slip along the bed rail. There was about half a dozen people close by. Someone must have noticed his foot up there in full view but no-one commented. He didn't expect that kind of reaction, he had visualised himself as centre of attraction with everyone crowding round to marvel at him for daring to bring 'civvy' gear back off leave. He thought someone might even have asked to try them on.

He didn't want to bring the subject up himself, he wanted to appear casual although the suspense was driving him crazy.

'Oh well, things to do,' he mumbled.

Nobody looked up so he started back toward his bed when he noticed Dereham for the first time. Dereham must have come back on the same train and come in on the same bus, but Ginger hadn't noticed him until now. This was it. Dereham would notice and his loud voice would ensure that everyone else knew. Yes, Dereham would soon make him centre of attention.

'Hi yah, Dereham,' he greeted Dereham in what he hoped wasn't a too obvious false attempt at friendliness. 'Had a good leave then?'

As before he cocked his foot up but this time he put it right in the middle of Dereham's bed. He couldn't help but see the new plimsoles.

'What's up wiv you then? An' get yer foot off my bed. Ain't you got nuffink to do. Sod off.'

Apparently Dereham hadn't had a very good leave.

That was the last straw.

If Dereham didn't notice then probably no-one would. He had brought those plimsoles back partly out of bravado because he knew it was not allowed. He thought he might wear them after supper when Leverett and Jury had left for the night; he might even risk wearing them to the CMG for breakfast sometimes.

That would be a laugh. That chap from 49 mess wearing his 'civvy' plimsoles right under the noses of the instructors, they would say. Pretty soon everyone would know he had a pair of illegal plimsoles. Everyone except the instructors of course. The word would spread and boys from other messes, perhaps other divisions, would come to look at him.

He ambled up and down the mess a couple of time to give them another chance to notice his feet, but as no-one showed any interest he decided to try his luck down below in the colonnade. Others would still be returning from leave and someone was sure to notice him.

He certainly got noticed all right. But it didn't have quite the same effect that he had dreamed of.

'That boy there.'

There was no mistaking that nasal growl. He had run slap bang into Batchelor. He should have known better. In his enthusiasm to show off the footwear that was going to make him the talk of the place, he had forgotten about Batchelor. He should have known Batchelor would be there. Batchelor was always there. That nasty so-and-so quite probably came back off his own leave early so that he would be there when the boys returned.

There was no getting away from him, the colonnade was empty and he was well and truly caught.

'Report to me.'

Back off leave about ten minutes and the first person to take any notice of him just had to be bloody Batchelor. He had craved attention but this was not a bit like what he had in mind.

'What's that on your feet.'

Having just come from home where people treated you as an equal and not yet fully back into Ganges routine, Ginger felt brave enough to try and brazen it out.

'It's my plimsoles, sir. My mum must have packed them by mistake. I thought I would just wear them tonight until I sort my kit out sir.'

The thin ringer stood in his usual pose, hands behind his back, leaning slightly forward and that horrible scowl was on his face. He was not impressed.

'Take them off,' he rasped, holding his hand out for them.

Ginger was beaten.

He was beaten from the moment Batchelor first saw him. He had felt brave enough to answer back. But he was beaten. He felt that he might just as well answer back while he had the nerve to do so. Those kind of feelings didn't last long in Ganges.

He took off his treasured possessions and handed them over and at the same time felt his fantasy crumble inside him. He had brought his plimsoles in and no-one had seen them. No-one except Batchelor that was. To make matters worse he had spent seven shillings of his leave pay on them and within minutes they were gone—gone forever.

Bloody Batchelor had done it again.

The following morning Batchelor was in the colonnade when they fell in for their first muster after breakfast.

There was nothing unusual about that really. He turned up for every muster so that the instructors could report to him before marching their classes away to their various activities. But this time Ginger felt sure that his eyes were on him.

Although Ginger's class was the nearest to the swimming bath and Batchelor was right down the other end he felt his eyes were on him, boring right into him. He could sense the staring and he couldn't help looking back. Every time he tried a crafty glance, he caught the thin ringers eye; it was not imagination. Batchelor was staring at him.

PO Jury, their duty instructor, was last to report and as he turned about to return to the class, Batchelor followed him, his eyes seemed to be fixed on

Ginger all the time. He was in the centre rank but Batchelor was looking straight at him.

'You need a haircut,' he thundered.

He was still some distance off and it was doubtful if he was able to tell from that far away. It was a pretty safe bet anyway because, having just returned from leave, none of them had their hair cut for at least three weeks. But why had he singled out Ginger as the only one among three hundred boys that were in front of him defied logic. Maybe it was something to do with the plimsole episode of the previous afternoon; maybe he was on another of his power surges. Where Batchelor was concerned, who could tell.

He walked right up close and pushed in between the boys in the front rank, to stand directly in front of him.

'You boy. Get your hair cut. How dare you show yourself on my parade with hair in that condition,' he spat the words right in Ginger's face.

They normally had their hair cut every two weeks but having been on leave for the past three weeks, it was certain to be a bit longer than usual. But so was everyone else's. They had all got at least three weeks growth but he had only singled out Ginger.

'Get it cut as soon as possible and don't let me see you in that state ever again,' he snarled, stepping back to let the front rank close up again.

Ginger knew his hair wasn't that bad. PO Jury made no comment. Jury didn't like any of his boys to be singled out, he looked upon it as 'letting the class down' but this time he said nothing. He would never openly criticise another instructor but his face, for once, showed an emotion. It showed he didn't agree with Batchelor.

After the mid-morning stand-easy they mustered in the colonnade once more. Batchelor was there.

As soon as the boys started to drift down, he made a beeline straight for Ginger.

'That boy there.'

Although he had a deep nasal voice he could be loud when the occasion demanded. It put all kinds of fear into them all. The milling throngs of boys all stood still and all the chattering stopped as they looked round to see which of them he was addressing.

Ginger didn't need to look. He knew.

Before he could run over to report to the officer, Batchelor had covered the ground between them and they were face to face in a flash; he had that sadistic grin on his face.

Ginger swallowed hard, he'd seen that grin before. His short life flashed before him.

'I thought I told you to get a haircut.'

Well give me a chance, Ginger thought to himself. But he had been caught flatfooted and low on bravado.

He replied meekly: ' Yes sir.'

Something was going on in that evil mind. That grin was still on Batchelor's face, he was enjoying humiliating a boy in front of everyone. The grin, which was not much different from his snarl, was his attempt at humour. It was a false patronising smile to let everyone know he was joking. Ginger knew better. So did the majority of people under that colonnade.

'Maybe I can help you to remember,' he said loudly.

He drew a biro pen from his inside pocket then, grabbing Ginger's head, he scribbled blue ink down each side of his face, in front of the ears.

There was not a sound to be heard. A Petty Officer from one of the other messes started forward but then changed his mind and averted his eyes.

Ginger felt sick.

The feelings from that first meal in the Annexe came flooding back, but this time he held his composure. He refused to let Batchelor see any emotion, he wouldn't give him the satisfaction. He felt emotional but he was determined not to show it; he stared expressionless straight back into the thin ringer's face.

If he had the power to will anyone dead, Batchelor would have been a pile of putrefied slime at his feet.

The next period was seamanship and as Leverett was not there, Batchelor would take them down to the seamanship block.

After a curt: 'Carry on Petty Officer,' as a way of dismissing Jury, he marched them out of the colonnade and on to the bottom road.

They marched down the hill parallel with Collingwood until suddenly— 'Class halt.'

They stood still waiting for his next order, wondering what was going on.

'That boy.'

Ginger caught his eye.

'Report to me.'

Now the penny dropped. They were outside the barbers shop. There was a grassy bank leading up to the door and Batchelor strode up it purposefully.

'Follow me,' he instructed.

Ginger fell out and followed him.

Inside, two barbers were busy and several people, ships company probably, were sitting waiting their turn.

'Wait there.'

Batchelor indicated that he should remain standing and wait by the door. Then, as the first chair became vacant he stepped forward putting his hand on it.

'Sit there.'

He ignored people waiting, never giving them as much as a second glance. Ginger stepped forward slowly, reluctant to jump the queue and half expecting some objection to be raised. Batchelor roughly grabbed his arm to hurry him along and pushed him into the seat.

The civilian barber made no comment as he draped the cloth around Ginger's shoulders. He made no comment when Batchelor angrily tore it away.

The electric clippers buzzed into life and he felt them power up the back of his head.

'That's enough,' declared Batchelor.

The barber could take no more.

'You can't leave him looking like that,' he said, jumping to Ginger's defence.

Batchelor's face looked as black as thunder.

'That's enough, I said.'

'Fall in outside with the rest of the class,' he snarled, addressing Ginger.

By that time the humiliation had subsided and he no longer cared. He left the chair, haircut unfinished and joined the rest of the class at the bottom of the slope. He had no alternative but to obey in any case but the barber was not governed by any such restrictions and he was far from finished.

Even at that distance the boys could clearly hear the pair of them arguing, they were going at it hammer and tongs and very nearly out of control. Ginger hoped the barber would punch him.

They would love to see Batchelor rejoin them with a black eye or a bloody nose, but no such luck. Although he had met someone who was not afraid to stand up to him, that evil little Kraut had come out on top again.

It hurt to know that Batchelor had got away with his sadistic trickery once more but now that his humiliation and frustration had left him, Ginger didn't care. He left the unfinished haircut as it was right round until after tea before he went back to have it finished off.

He'd been home on leave, so he wasn't a nozzer in the strictest sense of the word any longer.

He was an old hand and he could take whatever they threw at him.

He vowed that none of these Navy bastards would ever upset him again.